Contents

IN DEBT
CANT PAY
DON'T PAY

What Happens When You Stop Paying Your Credit Card Debt

Charles V. Jerome

3050523 24917 116

Copyright © LiteraryCat.org 2023
All rights reserved. No part of this book may be reproduced except for fair comment or review without written permission from the author or the publishers.
I would love to hear from you.
My email address is at the end of this book.
or via my associates' website

LiteraryCat.org

Contents

Disclaimer.

As I am not legally qualified. I recommend that you seek a legal professional when dealing with points of law. They may suggest a more conservative approach than mine, which involves negotiating with the creditor and paying them with funds that are not currently available and subsequently paying their fees from the same funds that are also not currently available.

However, you should note that this may not always be in your best interests, as such advice to protect you may also be given to limit the lawyer's liability.

Try to find an adviser or lawyer who will work pro-bono (without charge); they are good people and they are out there. And take this book with you.

It is still possible that following the advice provided in this book could still lead to litigation, nonetheless based on research and experience, it is highly improbable. My advice is given in good faith, based on experience, but without liability. I therefore cannot be held responsible for costs or damages however caused.

However, you are not on your own. If you have problems or would like to share your experience, or just chat, my email address and further advice are at the end of the book.

"There are two ways to conquer and enslave a nation. One is by the sword. The other is by debt."
John Adams, the second President of the United States

Contents

> **THE RICH RULE OVER THE POOR AND THE BORROWER IS A SLAVE TO THE LENDER.**
>
> **PROVERBS 22.7**

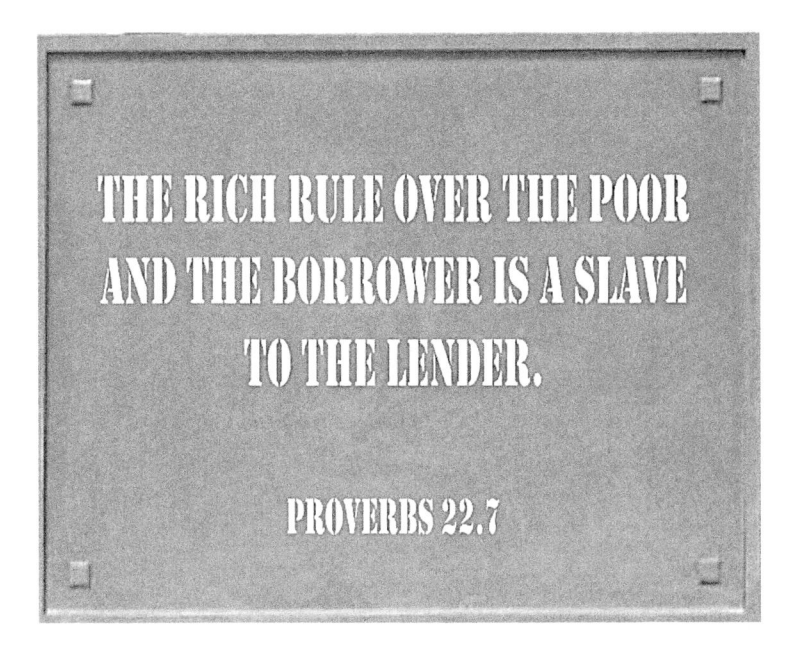

Debt collection is a multi-billion-dollar industry that preys on the most vulnerable members of society."
Jesse Jackson, American civil rights leader

What is this book about? If you're struggling with a credit card or an unsecured bank loan, you may arrive in a situation where you have to make a choice - you could eat or pay the banker's monthly fees - you can't do both.

I am assuming you may have contacted various organisations working to help people in debt.
In the UK for example there is Stepchange Debt Charity, National Debtline and Payplan, and of course, the Citizens Advice Bureau. Check the internet for similar organisations in the USA and the EU
All offer advice on how to *manage* your debt. They may even contact creditors directly and negotiate a reduced monthly

payment on your behalf – the upshot is you are in debt for a lot longer. They dare not advise on how to eradicate your debt, forever, as I do. That I understand.
Super, so you spend the next decade paying off the bankers to maintain their profit levels. You cut back on all those things you wanted, but can't because you 'must' make repayments at interest rates you can't afford. You 'do without' because that's your station in life.

Yes, sure, you should not have got into debt. But you did. It was a trap. It was so easy Bankers want you to get into debt, it's lucrative, followed by debt collection agencies, followed by credit rating agencies – another massive industry trading in debt.

(I will though most of this book call the practitioners of the debt industry the 'bankers' to include credit card companies, store cards and bank loans to save repetition and constant cross-referencing.)

The head bankers are paying themselves millions a year, while you have a debt you can't pay, a debt that's increasing, a misery, a prison, a hell

Think of another option…
What if you chose not to pay? And then what?
Does the sky fall in on you? No.
Are you thrown in jail? No.
Do you eat? Yes.

Yes, there will be flack!
Stand firm. They will use several weapons to get at you, both physiological: fear, threats and social conditioning; the shame of being in debt – you will not succumb to fear and the shame is on them, not you.

Contents

The law is more on your side than you think. I will prove that bankers have become scurrilous, dishonest extortionists and you deserve the right to say no.

First, the bankers will use every threat they can think of to scare you. When that doesn't work, after about a month or so, they sell the 'debt' (funded by the money they created from thin air - see chapter six) to a debt collection agency. The greedy agency.

The debt collectors pile in with the same threats, a rush of gluttony to get some money, any money, from you. Their only tool is fear.

If you allow yourself to succumb to the harassment and intimidation rather than face them off, they will perceive you as weak. When they sense fear, they also sense capitulation and become more aggressive - drooling at the thought of collecting hard-earned cash for an account they only paid a few percent for.

Face them off, and turn their arguments against them – and there are plenty to use; I'll show you how. They will give up and not spend time chasing a debt already proven to be worthless.

The most likely thing to happen is, after all the letters, threats, hot air and bluffing, they leave you alone - you both walk away. You have the freedom, the joy, to start again. They are free to create more debt.

That is what this book is about, your guide to the liberation of debt.

Money is a new form of slavery, and distinguishable from the old simply by the fact that it is impersonal - that there is no human relation between master and slave."
Leo Tolstoy

Contents

Chapter one Welcome 8
    The stress of debt 13
Chapter Two The world is in debt 17
    You are not alone 17
    What is Debt? 22
Chapter Three You will win 27
Chapter five Banking Ethics 33
    Bankers manipulate the debt markets 33
    Extortion? 35
    Dirty Hands – bankers? 38
Chapter Six: Banks Create Money from Thin Air 40
    Then charge you interest on the phantom money. 40
Chapter Seven   Debt Liberation Day 46
    Your credit agreement – complexities arguments 53
    Always avoid answering direct questions. 60
    What if the bank or agency asks you to complete a 'financial audit'? 62
Chapter Eight The debt collection agency 66
Credit Rating Agencies 81
Chapter Nine Statute of Limitations 85
    In a nutshell. 88
Chapter Ten Bankers & Robbers 89

Contents

    Banks Cheating on Their Customers. 89

    Wells Fargo fake accounts scandal (2016): 92

    The 2008 subprime mortgage crisis 94

Yarns of banks & cards & other bits 97

    Harry and the Story of Multiple Card Debts 97

    Peter, the HSBC & the Gizmo 101

Chapter Twelve Epilogue 105

Further Reading 110

Notes 116

Chapter one

Welcome

I am assuming two scenarios occasioned you to read these first pages.

1) You are in debt to a credit card company or a bank via an unsecured loan; your card is maxed out, you can't pay, or you are struggling to pay, the interest is compounding, and the fines are mounting. You are looking for a way out that works with the minimum of trauma.
2) Or you realise that is a situation you could be in one day and would not know what to do about it.
3) Or you are just curious and would like to know more about going up against the goliaths of capitalist society – the banks.

Is that what interested you in this book? Read on; I have good news on the first two counts - and items of interest, enough for you to alter your perception in the third.

Yes, I am serious, in the title and sub-title - if you can't pay, then don't pay.

From the personal experience of friends, and friends of friends, who shared their experiences with me and researching - every time, after some carefully worded replies to the banks and credit card companies plus an understanding of the shadowy world of the debt market - the vampires, the leeches - you will be left alone.

Two things you need. The information and guidance in this book and determination. You will take a battering from the bankers and the debt agency. Intimidation and bullying is

Chapter one
Welcome

their profession, their weapon, and they are good at it.
So be prepared.

Ready for a skirmish? Let's start. And it won't be difficult and you will win.

I shall use Jane as the figurative victim of debt.
And I shall use Bob Diamond, ex-CEO of Barclays Bank UK, who resigned after a scandal, as the epitome of a greedy, spiritually ugly banker.

Jane is a single mother with one child to feed and clothe. She is in despair. She was just scraping by financially. She had used her credit card before and mostly managed to pay each month. But things were getting tougher; costs were rising, food, electricity and rent. All were becoming more expensive.

A year ago, she could not make ends meet. She just needed some credit to get by, just for a month or two, just this time, this time only she promised herself. Set the direct debit repayments to a minimum. The trap was sprung.

As the months passed, there was the dawning unpalatable truth that there was nothing spare to pay back the debt.

A year came and went. She is now deeply in debt. Not only does she have her cost of living to find, but she has to service exorbitant interest rates and fines when she is late paying. Being punished with a fine because you cant pay is as absurd as it is cruel. So she is slipping further into debt while the bankers get richer.

She is suffering. She can't sleep; she is distressed every minute of the day. She feels trapped; that's because she is trapped. Debt is a prison.

Chapter one
Welcome

Eventually and inevitably, her card is maxed out. She not only has that extra monthly expense to service, but she has no more credit available to pay for unseen emergencies.

Jane initially felt shame and disgrace for her situation. However, Bob Diamond just felt another $750,000 stuffed into his pocket and had no remorse. I hope to change the perception of good and bad for Jane from within this book, give her dignity, and set her free from her current debt.

How did it get this way?

"The world is a stage, and in our Lifetime we play many parts."
Paraphrased from Shakespeare

During our life, we may have oscillated between rich and poor and between abundance and lack. What you don't want, what we don't need when finances are tight, is to be forced to borrow at high interest to the point of no return. The nagging horror that you will slip so far behind and not be able to pay and forever stay in debt.

Forever is a long, long time.

Hence this book. I will show you how to eliminate credit card debts and unsecured bank loans. Quickly, methodically, and you will - without any remorse or guilt. The opposite! The bankers showed no regret for your situation. Their motivation is greed They encourage debt. Debt is their business, and it does not matter who suffers.

Ridding current debt will give you breathing space and an opportunity to start again and make better plans.

I have kept this book to just over 100 pages, about two hours, and informative with the advice you need while also keeping

Chapter one
Welcome

the price affordable. If you are in debt, I don't expect you to shell out a premium figure for its purchase.

Annual income twenty pounds, annual expenditure nineteen and six, result happiness. Annual income twenty pounds, annual expenditure twenty pounds and six, result misery."
Charles Dickens

Debt is a disease. I will show you, step by step, how to dump your debt and cure this disease. That's the relatively easy part. The tricky part is convincing you that the bankers, card companies and debt collectors are the tyrants, not you. Maybe you already know that.

You will beat them at their own game. Legal words and bluffing, threats and bluster are two-way.

I can't say the banks will be happy. But, on the other hand, they will not be unhappy. They just don't care. They have no emotion; for them, it's business; and your debt, paid up or not, is still an asset that can be traded. The interest when you were paying - and the charges to retailers - made it a lucrative business.

When a banker makes a loan, they 'create' a deposit for the borrower, which is then recorded as an asset on the bank's balance sheet - effectively creating money from nothing – more on that in chapter six.

They won't even shrug their shoulders when you stop paying because dumping the debt has already been factored in and probably insured. They then sell your debt to a debt collection agency. Nice business.

They can't lose. The good news for you is the countdown for the statute of limitations also started ticking when you stopped paying.

Chapter one
Welcome

Sure, you will have a bad credit score for a few years. But you will have that anyway if you can't pay. Live with it for now; there are ways around it – read the section on credit rating in chapter ten.

What I am offering is the ridding of your current debt and the monthly payments now, this moment. That will get you on your feet again, an opportunity to start living again.

Use the emotional energy you were wasting on your debt and redirect that incredible energy we all possess to a better purpose, creating new enterprises and attitudes – we all deserve better than the claustrophobic burden of unpayable debt.

Unless you have inherited a couple of hundred million and are sensible, your equity comfort level and level of debt will vary all your life, first as a student, then as a parent, and then as a pensioner. Slowly, things may start to go wrong, so you turn to your credit card. Your 'Flexible Friend' as one of the credit card (Access) advertising themes went.

Then you're really in debt. You're starting to live in subjugation. Week by week, day by day, hour by hour in debt.

You dreaded the postman when he knocked with a recorded delivery.

That is not the way to live.

Chapter one
Welcome

The stress of debt

United States:
A study published in the American Journal of Preventive Medicine in 2016 found that people with debt were more than twice as likely to attempt suicide as those who did not have debt. The study also found that the risk of suicide increased with the level of debt.

United Kingdom:
A study published in the Journal of Epidemiology and Community Health in 2013 found that people with debt were more than three times as likely to have suicidal thoughts as those who did not have debt.

What can you do?
Make more money and pay off your debt. Cool, yes, in a perfect world.
Borrow from friends and family. Bad idea! It could lead to friction, and you will still be in debt.

Check with your country's Citizens Advice Bureau. They should be sympathetic and may be able to advise where and how you could obtain benefits.

Or, I will show you how to dump your bank loan and card debt. Walk away without paying a single penny and with no regret for the bankers. Then, start again, start afresh. How will you feel with those card and bank debts out of the way?

That is why I wrote this book.

What have you to lose by following my advice? Your fear? Fear is their weapon, and the only thing they can threaten you with is going to court. And that, believe me, is very, very unlikely. The bankers are, if nothing else (and they are

Chapter one
Welcome

probably nothing else), realists and pragmatists. Read the stories/case histories at the end of this book.

Bankers don't give a hoot about you. Never did. Similarly, you should not grieve over the bank when you follow my advice. If the debt proves too much effort to enforce, they will drop it. (And I will show you with legal arguments how to make it too much effort to enforce.)

When you don't pay, no worries for them, they have insurance. The costs of a delinquent account are already factored in. At first, your account is called delinquent. When they write off the account it's called 'in default' (more on that later). They know there is little point in trying to get blood out of a stone. Then, still not giving a hoot about you, they will sell it to a debt collecting agency or, if they think you have some assets you are hiding, i.e., cash or property worth attacking, they will keep the debt on their books and instruct an agency to work on their behalf. That won't be your situation.

That's great. The agency - all bluster and sabre-rattling - will then try to… well, read on. Follow this book, take the correct actions, ask the correct, niggling questions, and slowly the agency, the bankers, and the card companies will leave you and the debt alone, forever.

It's well on its way to a place called oblivion. By the time you finish this book, your life will start to look a lot better.

Chapter Seven is the day you decide not to pay. That's it. Follow the advice I give from experience. Sure, there are procedures to go through - at your pace, not theirs. Simply, stop paying.

This will work 95% of the time. Of course, I can't give you a mathematical certainty; percentages quoted like this are based

Chapter one
Welcome

on guesswork, not fact, and thus can only be regarded as a cliché, not the literal odds. Nonetheless, the odds, even metaphorical, are vastly in your favour.

Debt is a prolific mother of folly and of crime.
Benjamin Disraeli

I have set out to keep this book as short, concise, and easy to assimilate as possible - with maybe some humour, and anecdotes. I have also used illustrations. Not to make it pretty but to add easily found placemarks. Also, as you will become aware, I would like to stimulate your imagination, to regain the spirit you lost when succumbing to debt. An illustration can, within seconds, convey a depth of feeling that would otherwise take a hundred words.

Books have two purposes: to entertain or to inform. Sometimes both. I hope both.

You have information within this book, information that will change your life. Gain a breathing space. Knowing and comprehending how the banks and card industries work and think is the key to succeed. Knowing this, knowing their evil 'game' is the way you will beat them and not pay a dime, a cent or a penny in doing so.

A few notes.

I am English. My experience is with British and some European laws. However, the principles of civil laws and processes are very similar in most of Europe and the USA.

As I said in my disclaimer, I am not a lawyer, solicitor, accountant, or financial adviser. However, I have had personal experience with the implementation of the strategies in this book.

Almost every time, by following my guidance based on observations and experience, you will cleanse yourself of debts incurred by unsecured loans, credit/store cards, and greedy bankers.

Not 100% of the time, as above, but nearer 95%.

> *If you can't pay anyway, you have little else to lose - and little else to lose is a risk worth taking*
> *CVJ*

I also had to choose between eating and paying exorbitant rates of interest. I relate to that choice, eating or paying several times in this book. Not to be smart, but because it was true. If I had continued paying monthly card bills, the repayments meant nothing was left for the supermarket. I chose to eat.

I won. I dumped all my credit card debts on that goods wagon, watched it leave, waved goodbye, and started living again.

I have advised friends and friends of friends in similar circumstances. I have researched first-hand accounts of people who have said, "Enough is enough", and stopped paying and then what happens?

Read on.

Chapter Two
The world is in debt

Chapter Two

The world is in debt

You are not alone
And neither are you on your own.

How many people in the West are behind with credit card payments?

As described earlier, there are three stages your account enters when you don't pay:

Delinquent. This is usually declared by the bank or card company around 30 days after your payment went overdue. **Default,** the bank declares an account as 'in default' when they have sold it to a debt collection agency or have otherwise written it off. In other words, they have nothing to do with it anymore—usually between 90 and 180 days. **In Collection** is the term used by debt collection agencies when they have acquired (bought) the debt and are pursuing it on their own behalf.

The status of all the above is reported to the credit rating agencies by bankers as and when your account changes status.

Do you own a credit card?
Or does the credit card own you?
CVJ

Consistent statistics, for the total amount of credit card debt per country or nation are mysteriously hard to find.

Chapter Two
The world is in debt

This is mainly because those statistics are reports issued by credit rating agencies and then collated for statistical research by bankers and government agencies. And statistics like these tend to be subjective.

For example, a political party that was in power at the time could manipulate how these statistics are presented. A new government coming into office may want to show the previous government as inept by allowing the debt figure to rise, while an incumbent government leaving office would instead show how well they have done in keeping consumer debt down.

With some extrapolation/interpolation, averaging, common-sense and guess work I have produced the figures below

The following are based on stats compiled in and around 2021/2022
With rising inflation and interest rates rising globally, the default rate and average debt per cardholder will be somewhat higher, methinks a lot higher, at the time of this book's publication.

USA
The United States of America had a population during this time of 332 million. Of that, 76%, or 252.3 million, owned a credit card (source: American Bankers Association)
According to Experian, the multinational consumer credit reporting company, the average credit card debt was $5,315.)
The delinquency rate was 1.64%, and the default rate was 2.47%
(source: Federal Reserve Bank of St. Louis)

As the delinquency rate is transient, around three months until it has either been paid off or sold, the fair measure of

Chapter Two
The world is in debt

the number of people who could not pay their credit card is the default rate.

That was 2.47% meaning 6.2 million people had defaulted on their cards in this period.

UK
The United Kingdom had a population of 68 million. Of that, 60%, or 40.8 million, owned a credit card. According to a 2020 report by, The Money Charity, the average credit card debt per household in the United Kingdom was £2,590.
According to the Bank of England's Money and Credit report for August 2021, the credit card default rate in the UK was 5.1% or just over 2 million. These figures seem confirmed by the Bank of England, although they seem to be double that of the USA and three times that of the EU.

The EU.
The European Union is not a single country but a political and economic union of 27 member states (as of 2021, its estimated population was around 447 million people. However, according to a 2020 report by the European Central Bank, credit card penetration rates in the Eurozone (the 19 EU member states that use the euro as their currency) range from around 10% in cash-dependent countries like Germany and Austria to over 80% in countries like Belgium and Finland.

According to the same study, approximately 65% or over 290 million people in the European Union own at least one credit card. (That would include, at that time, before Brexit, the UK).
From the same study, the average credit card debt in the

Chapter Two
The world is in debt

Eurozone (the 19 EU member states that use the euro as their currency) was around €1,385. However, it's worth noting that high credit card usage rates heavily influenced this figure in countries like Belgium and Finland, where average credit card debt can be significantly higher.

It was also assessed that the average default rate was 1.5%, although reliable figures for the average of all member states are hard to confirm. But that average looks like a reasonable estimate. So, a simple calculation based on rough estimates shows that 4.35 million accounts were in default.

Hence, we have the total number of credit card holders in default in 2021/22 as:

- UK: 2 million.
- EU 4.35 million.
- USA 6.2 million.
- Total in 2021/22 - 12.55 million

That's over 12 million people who could not keep up with credit card payments. A lot of people suffering because of debt.
And those figures were compiled a few years ago. The global economy has declined a lot since then. Those numbers could be double today.

You are not alone. And you are not on your own. CBS News recently reported that nearly six in 10 Americans (41%) don't have enough savings to cover a $500 unplanned expense. That means when these unexpected bills come along- how are they paid – via credit card, personal loan or borrowing from friends or family?

Chapter Two
The world is in debt

The first two options would be drowning more people in high-interest debt, and the third could create a problematic situation.

This is an increasing debt crisis that the blood-hounds of the debt-collecting agencies are drooling over

With global inflation rising and another recession's spectra on the horizon, people are worried.

Adding to the gloom are more bank meltdowns through criminal incompetence, like the collapse of the Silicon Valley Bank, which went bust at the time of this book's publication. As one bank goes down or needs bailing out, the knock-on effects are the destruction of business and loss of jobs. This was a bank financing startup enterprises, people lost more than just money; people lost their dreams. Debt is a society under the whip. A society under control. The poor are subservient to the rich.

With the global economy still recovering from the Covid pandemic, the central banks needed to print more money so governments could pay bills leading to the devaluing of currency, fuelling inflation and sending the cost-of-living rocketing to crisis point.

Interest rates are jacked up to curb spending, meaning less money is circulating, thereby controlling inflation caused by the said printing of more money. A spiral of events is destroying lives – and, of course, the banks make more money as borrowing intensifies, and interest rates rise.

And who is the end consumer of the higher interest rates? We are - via credit cards, personal loans and mortgages. Borrowers are forced to increase their borrowing to pay higher interest rather than using the money to reduce their debt.

Chapter Two
The world is in debt

The poor with debts get poorer, while the rich with assets get richer.

The most numbing statistics from the web - the total private citizen's indebtedness in the USA for all debts, in 2022 was $16.9 trillion, and of that credit card debt was $1.1 trillion.

What is Debt?

That is not quite such a naive question. Analyse the meaning and types of debt and loan interest.

How do we acquire money to pay bills and shop when things are tight?

Chapter Two
The world is in debt

Borrowing from Friends and Relatives?
If you borrowed from a friend or relative, that debt must be re-paid in good faith and in swift order. "Neither a borrower nor a lender be." is a famous line from Hamlet.

The full quote is:

> *"Neither a borrower nor a lender be, for loan oft loses both itself and friend."*

Good advice for if debts linger, resentment on both sides' festers. A financially poor friend borrowing from a more affluent friend leads to bitterness – both from the poor friend for the perceived shame of having to borrow and from the richer friend who starts to feel used if, or as, the repayment is delayed. If you are fortunate to have a good friend or relative willing and able to lend, re-pay as soon as possible.
It's more than a priority. It's your duty.

> *Most religions are opposed to interest on personal loans.*

While there is no explicit prohibition on charging interest in the Bible, moral concerns exist regarding exploiting the poor and the vulnerable through lending practices. In some cases, Christian denominations of all types have promoted ethical lending practices that prioritise the well-being of borrowers over profit.

We know the story of Jesus overturning the moneylenders' tables.
I quote:

> *And as he taught them, he said, "Is it not written: My house will be called a house of prayer for all nations'?*
> *But you have made it a den of robbers'"*
> *(Mark 11:17)"*

Chapter Two
The world is in debt

Interesting that he refers to the money lenders, i.e., the bankers - as robbers.

The Bible has several verses that address the ethics of charging interest on personal loans. Here are some examples:

"If you lend money to any of my people with you who is poor, you shall not be like a moneylender to him, and you shall not exact interest from him."
Exodus 22:25

"Take no interest from him or profit, but fear your God that your brother may live beside you."
Leviticus 25:36-37

"He who increases his wealth by interest and usury gathers it for him who is generous to the poor."
Proverbs 28:8

"Do not charge a fellow Israelite interest, whether on money or food or anything else that may earn interest." -
Deuteronomy 23:19-2

The Quran and the hadiths make it clear that interest is an exploitative practice. This doctrine, called Riba, is primarily respected by about a quarter of the global population against the concept of charging to lend money.

The Hebrew Bible (Torah) also prohibits charging interest on loans between fellow Jews (Deuteronomy 23:19-20), although some forms of interest are allowed when dealing with non-Jews.

Buddhist teachings emphasise the importance of compassion, generosity, and non-exploitation.
Charging excessive interest or exploiting the vulnerability of

Chapter Two
The world is in debt

borrowers through lending practices are inconsistent with Buddhist values.

It is worth noting that each religion has its unique perspective on the ethical concerns related to lending and interest. Moreover, these perspectives can vary widely depending on the context and interpretation.

And, of course, the humanistic perspective; it is against common decency and honesty, charging exorbitant rates and penalties to those trapped in debt.

As you probably know, an oxymoron is a figure of speech in which contradictory terms appear in conjunction. Generosity and compassion become an oxymoron when discussing the current practice of banks and credit card money lenders. Lending at exorbitant interest rates, sometimes at more than ten times the rate of the MLR, is evil. Adding fines for late payment when you are already struggling is evil. Selling the debt to a collection agency when you are desperately stressed and unable to pay is anything but 'generosity and compassion', mainly when the banks and card companies usually receive insurance for 'bad' debts after 90 days.

More on that later…

If you are starting a commercial enterprise, borrowing at a fair interest rate is sound business sense for both the borrower and the lender.
However, this is usually only entertained if the debt is 'secured', i.e., you pledge your house or other assets. If you are forming a Limited (LTD) or an INC (Incorporated) company, you may have to offer as we do in the UK 'Directors Guarantees´, pledging personal assets, your house, for example, to secure the loan.

Chapter Two
The world is in debt
But that's business. We are all grown up now.

Besides, interest paid is tax deductible. The contract should be fair on both sides, clearly written and understood and then we are set to go.

Chapter Three

You will win

All components of the banking world, the bankers, card companies and debt agencies, are realists and, for lack of a better word, lazy. Their business is profit. They only care about profit. We convince them that chasing an 'alleged debt' - from now on the debt is alleged - is not going to be profitable for them.

Knowing this and putting yourself in their shoes is how you will beat them. You have the moral right to cease paying – the high morals do not belong to the bankers, the agencies, and the bureaus. The collective word should be robbers. This is even more galling when you realise, they created the money for your loan as if by magic and then charged you interest essentially on the money you allowed them to create. See chapter six.
Shame on them not you.

How do you win against the massive banking institutions that seemingly have the moral high ground and the full weight of the law to back them?

Because I used the word 'seemingly'.

The profit motive overrides all other considerations when the bankers realise they have the spectra of wasting serious time involving senior staff, forcing them to answer reams of searching questions on the law. And then challenging their ethics, their methodology of threats and intimidation.

Chapter Three
You will win

This chapter is to convince you that you will beat the bankers and their lackeys, but more to the point, I want to reverse the social conditioning, so ingrained that you are doing something wrong. The banker's first motive is greed and their skills trickery. Their endgame when we say "enough is enough" is threats and bullying.

You have right on your side. You are taking back from the robbers what was not theirs in the first place.

(Check out chapter ten reference the immorality tricks, greed and often the incompetence of bankers.)

> *"Banking scandals are the price we pay for living in a capitalist society. The pursuit of profit at all costs creates a moral hazard that can never be eliminated."* -
> *Joseph Stiglitz*
> *American economist and professor at Columbia University*
> *Nobel Prize laureate in economics in 2001*

When you don't pay, they sell your debt to a Debt Collection Agency who are ungainly experts at harassment and intimidation.

Forget the pre-conditioned retorts of hell and damnation when you tell friends what you are planning. Show them this book. The bankers and their agencies have little to back them in law or morality – except the status quo, preconditioned social attitudes that belonged to another era.

Remember the bankers created free money for the 'loan'. They also filed your debt as an asset of the bank. They charged you an exorbitant rate of interest, plus fees and fines on late payments on the money they created from zero.

Chapter Three
You will win

They are then preparing to sell your debt to an agency. And then, as you read in chapter seven, get this - when you refuse to pay they have the nerve to write saying "Remember, we are here to help you manage your payments". The word 'remember' is just great. Also, the phrase, *'You must remember'*. Implying this is an inviolate fact and you are the one in error for not remembering it.

To continue: The banks either have insurance for bad debts or assume the risk themselves, which is paid for from the interest paid monthly by their clients. So, essentially, it was you who paid for the insurance, to compensate the maverick debt to the bank, for the money they conjured, that your default triggered.

And friends ask questions about *your* ethics?

Well done banks.

Check out other books on the subject of debt. Some suggest a more aggressive approach than I advocate. Picking on multiple points of law and banking ethics. Constantly probing and counter-arguing in an aggressive and confrontational manner. Battleground tactics of counter-threats and clever legal argument.

I suspect, in these situations, the creditors gave up pursuing the debt, considering it a waste of time rather than bowing down to clever legal wiles.
I also believe the chances of ending up in court are more probable because of an aggressive stance. To attack on every level, dismissing all the creditor's arguments, belittling their replies, and being ultra-smart on points of law is going to upset someone in head office.

Being right does not always win an argument. You must clarify the object of your discourse and work to that end. Take

Chapter Three
You will win

time to reason what 'winning' in this instant really means. Would you achieve the results you wanted from an aggressive approach? Maybe being clever scored some points, but point scoring could be very negative. When considering the human factor, it is more likely to land you in trouble than not. The metaphor 'winning the battle but losing the war' is apt here. (As regards winning - winning, what? I once played my future father-in-law chess. I won. Stupid move.)

Do you think if you upset someone in head office that you will be in a better situation? Especially if this is not the first time. You have, after all, in their eyes, reneged on a debt and that is almost sacrilegious to bankers.

When I was in business, my advice; was *"Making Enemies is expensive!"*. Ask if you can afford an enemy right now. Of course not.

Would it be better for you if there was someone sympathetic dealing with your case? Okay, probably hoping too much for sympathy, so let's go with at least indifference, rather than someone who has come to hate you with a vengeance for your confrontational approach. I do not recommend personally attacking those you are seeking not to pay. After the computer algorithms churn out stereotyped letters, it comes to one critical fact; it is a human who will make the final decision to take court action, or not, and the choice between someone they may even feel compassion for someone who is genuinely suffering and can't pay but has shown courtesy and respect - to that of a 'wide boy' exploiting the system, an amateur and cocky lawyer – I know which way I would vote. Through sheer and understandable bloody-mindedness, they may elect for litigation; just to teach a 'bad-ass' a lesson.

A good lawyer friend with lots of experience in litigation found that nearly always, with debts and other issues, the way

Chapter Three
You will win

to head off a confrontation is to offer what he termed *"The line of least resistance"*.

Give them an easy way out - walk away rather than fight - and it is human nature to take it. (lazy). Offer that to your creditors, the banks and card companies, in a tacit way – that they are best advised to follow the line of least resistance, save time and money and leave you alone.

Go to chapter seven for a draft of your first letters.

Treat bankers and agencies like a big brown bear sleeping at the entrance to our cave. Easy enough to sidestep and get away with it, a lot more difficult if you wake it up.

In love and debt – the gentlest gamester is the surest winner.
Plagiarised from Shakespeare

Rely on the principle that lending and, thus, debt is a tradeable business for banks, credit card companies and debt collectors. Accordingly, they will seek all ways to collect the debt or any part of it. They are in business to make money. They will give up if they see chasing as pointless and a waste of time.

That is what you will convince them to do.

Read on. I want you to get out of debt, even if you have multiple current debts, just this time, just this time only. And you almost certainly will if you follow my advice.

You apply the same tactics, play the same game with the agencies when or if your debt is 'handed over' (a polite word for hawked.) They will also take '*the line of least resistance*'; if that's all you offer; it's just business for them, it's prima-facie they have a useless debt and an extremely faint chance they could recover even part of it.

Don't worry; the agency has fewer powers than the bankers. In compensation, they turn up the bluffs, harassment and

Chapter Three
You will win

intimidation. See it as necessary pantomime. They have to try before they give up.

When they realise they are dealing with someone who understands enough law to fast-bowl awkward questions - and will not be intimidated - they will give up and stop wasting their time. They will let the debt sit there until the statute of limitations comes to an end – see chapter nine.

As we progress you will realise it is possible to 'milk the system to become a serial debtor. You will learn it is possible to obtain multiple cards in the future with no intention of ever paying.
(But note: If intent to seek a loan with no intention of paying can be proved, that becomes a criminal matter, not civil, and could lead to some very serious trouble.)
Yes, it is possible to continue in this vein, regain a positive credit rating, acquire new cards, and never paying back a cent. To argue your way out of every corner when the time comes.

It is possible.
Making a living this way is not good; it's negative; concentrate on creating something useful, not creating another round of debt and living in the murky world of the debt market that you have come to despise.

So, you think that money is the root of all evil. Have you ever asked what is the root of all money?
Ayn Rand,

Chapter five

Banking Ethics

**Bankers manipulate the debt markets
& destroy lives.**

*Man robs a bank and goes to prison.
Bank robs man, and bankers get a bonus.*
CVJ.

As you read in the previous chapter be aware of the banker's lack of ethics as you put in place the process of scrubbing your current debts, and don't feel bad. The whole industry must sort itself out, which will probably never happen since their profits exceed the fines for wrongdoing. Senior directors get huge bonuses even after doing a bad or crooked job – they are ruining the reputation of a business they were entrusted to govern - with diligence of course.

They are not the respectable institutions they once were—the opposite. So, I want you to feel no socially conditioned remorse, guilt, shame, fear or regret when going up against the greed of credit card companies and banks - just this once, which is for your sake, not theirs.

You were entering a trap the first day you appended your name to a piece of paper or clicked the button confirming your electronic signature to enter the devil's lair and sit at his table.

Maybe the trap lay dormant for years if you always paid in full each month. The teeth of the trap sprung the day you let the account go into the red. Now you are in the pockets of the

Chapter five
Banking Ethics

bankers and credit card dealers and maybe later the debt collection agencies.

They kept a straight face when they got you to sign the contract, the agreement.

They created money from nothing (see chapter six) then created your debt, and cashed in on the highest possible interest payment that the market would tolerate (and fines if you ever dared to be late paying).

We are going to turn the tables. You are going to renege on a palpably unfair contract.

"A contract that is fundamentally unfair or unjust may be unenforceable, even if it is technically valid."
LegalMatch.com

The way banks and credit card companies work are despicable, immoral, and probably the most significant case of extortion, a swindle, and outright robbery since the monitory system was conceived.

The general public is aware of this travesty but accepts it as the norm.

It's called 'social proofing' or 'social conditioning'.

The logic is in the belief that it must be okay if others are also willing to pay exorbitant interest and fines. It's okay if you pay monthly; you won't notice it at first. It's okay when banks via governments print money, that devalues the currency, triggering inflation (taxation by stealth) then shrug their shoulders at the mess the economy has become.

Social proofing says it's okay to accept the increased cost of living and the increased cost of borrowing and becoming the slave to debt - that everybody moans about, but everybody accepts —because that's the way it is and always was and will be.

Chapter five
Banking Ethics

The chains of habit are too weak to be felt until
they are too strong to be broken.
Samuel Johnson

The trap was set the day you signed the document; it fully closed when you realised you couldn't pay.

Yes, you are trapped.

In my opinion, and it should now be yours to consider, the banks and card companies are 'fair game' for your revenge. As the abused consumer, we have been induced to rack up a mountain of debt and live in a suffocating prison with no end; it's our turn to use the same tricks, the same sleight of hand, as they have used against us.

To prevent further clutter, I have moved the fables of the bank's shenanigans to the end of the book – chapter ten, Bankers & Robbers, a fascinating read.

I want you to understand that you are morally right and have a moral argument, to refuse further payments. Appreciate this before I tell you how to beat them.

Extortion?

For example, as of September 2021, the average credit card interest rate in the United States was around 16.03%, At that time the Federal Reserve Bank maintained its target range for the federal funds rate at 0.00% - 0.25%.

For simplicity let's call that 0.25% That is a markup of 6.420%

In the UK, the average credit card interest rate was around 17.9% in the same period. The Bank of England's Minimum Lending Rate (MLR) was 0.1% As banks arrange loans via interbank transactions, they will be borrowing very close to the MLR.

Chapter five
Banking Ethics

A markup of from 0.1% to 17.9% is 17,800% is extortion by any measure.

Sure, they have to factor in costs such as insurance to cover delinquent accounts. However, your debt is still worth cash as and when they sell it to a collection agency. Don't fret; they created that money from the ether by simply entering a debt into a ledger.

AND also realise credit card companies typically charge retailers a percentage of each transaction made using a credit card. This is known as the interchange fee or merchant discount rate, which can vary depending on the card network, the type of card used, and the merchant's industry.

When I was in retail, we offered American Express. They charged my company 6%. I gave very strict instructions to my staff not to offer Amex unless specifically requested. This was in the days when retailers used imprinting machines. We kept ours hidden.

On average, interchange fees range from around 1.5% to 3% of the transaction amount, although they can be higher for certain cards, such as premium or rewards cards. In addition, some credit card companies may also charge additional fees, such as processing, authorisation, or other monthly charges. Indeed, a win-win situation for the card company.

AND also realise that if you draw cash on your card, you could be charged around 2%.
(2% spot rate for a cash withdrawal when the annual interest rate was about that? And then they charge extortionate interest if you don't clear that at the end of the month) The bankers win, yet again, for the privileged of us receiving the loan in fiat* currency rather than goods.

Chapter five
Banking Ethics

*Fiat currency is the paper money issued by the government via the banks. With no gold standard, it has no value except the touching faith in banks and government that it does, in hope more than fact, have worth.

In the UK, in 2020, the average credit card spending per cardholder was around £8,000, according to data from UK Finance.

In the USA, the average credit card spending was around $10,000 for the same period, according to data from the Federal Reserve.

Let's go for the rate in dollars for this example. Say you have held a credit card for the past ten years. Inflation has been pretty gentle over the past decade, so we can ignore it now. Your spending via credit cards is thus ten years x $10,00 = $100,000. Assume an average cost to the retailer is 2.5%. Ignore those additional 'services' charged by the card companies that they levy on the retailer. In the past decade, the card company have, from your card alone, a gross profit of $2,500 and in the states alone there are 71 million credit card owners. If the averages are consistent that's $177.5 billion for the USA alone. Extrapolate those figures for the UK and the EU.

AND also realise that all costs to a retailer are eventually passed on to the customer. So, you pay indirectly to use your card on every purchase.

AND they will charge you, the end consumer, an exorbitant interest rate if you don't clear your account monthly. Also, depending on your country and the card you use, you may be charged an annual fee.

AND if you miss a single payment or are late, you will be fined, usually an eye-watering amount. And all this (as I discuss later) for a contract that starts life legally dubious.

Chapter five
Banking Ethics

Dirty Hands – bankers?
A legal term is used in litigation by one side or the other, saying that the opposing side comes to court with 'dirty hands.'
The term is a recognised legal expression used to describe a situation in which a party involved in a lawsuit was found to have acted unethically, fraudulently, or with wrongful intentions in the matter under dispute.

When one party accuses the other of 'coming to court with dirty hands' they are essentially alleging that the other party is not entitled to seek legal remedies or relief because they have engaged in wrongful or unethical conduct related to the dispute.

A contract must be fair and reasonable at the time it is made, and must not be so one-sided as to be oppressive or unconscionable to one party.
New York State Unified Court System

Essentially, the 'dirty hands' doctrine prevents a party from benefiting from their wrongful or unethical behaviour. It is a principle often used to deny relief or damages to a party who acted improperly in the matter at hand.
Certainly unethical, and taken to the precise meaning of contract laws – then illegal.

This could be useful when it is our turn to bluff.

Your friendly bank manager?
In almost every country, the days when we knew our bank manager by their first name and they knew ours - and would take time to chat, are all but gone.
Banking has become impersonal; they are just interested in profit, and more profit, and more profit after that.

Chapter five
Banking Ethics

Years ago, back in the seventies I think, there used to be a TV advertisement for one of the central banks about how they would help their customers.
It portrayed a customer, worried about a problem, then going to a cupboard to get out the bank manager who was waiting there, smart, smiling and ready to help, briefcase in hand!
(GrahamHancock.com forums)

What rot! The manager in the cupboard, that is.

No longer can you discuss a problem with your friendly high street bank. Instead, contact is via a call centre, probably in another country, with the staff reading from a script – if you can get hold of someone – or you are left hanging on to listen to irritating music. Or a crude attempt to engage you with open-source AI software. – often not artificial intelligence but AS, 'Artificial Stupidity.

Next chapter – the magic trick – how banks create money.

Chapter Six:

Banks Create Money from Thin Air

Then charge you interest on the phantom money.

> *It is well enough that people of the nation do not understand our banking and monetary system, for if they did, I believe there would be a revolution before tomorrow morning."*
>
> ***
>
> *The modern banking system manufactures money out of nothing. The process is perhaps the most astounding piece of sleight of hand that was ever invented.*
> *Henry ford.*

It is called the 'fractional reserve'. When a bank creates your account, it also creates a debt on a piece of paper, or electronically, adding this to the bank ledger as an asset. The crafty bit is the banker has only to fork up a percentage of the total loan granted from the bank's cash reserves for your loan. Thus, it is called a 'fractional' reserve. This can often be as low as 10%. They are then free to loan the difference i.e., in this case, 90%, to other pundits; also entered on the bank's ledger as an asset - thus creating money where no money existed. They then charge interest on the money that did not exist; that started its existence when the security document

Chapter Six:
Banks Create Money from Thin Air

was signed by you – and add-infinitum. Interest on phantom money continues every time debts are created – very slick.

The bank hath benefit of interest on all money, which it creates out of nothing.
William Paterson, one of the co-founders of the Bank of England.

This is all about loans and, thus, debts.

When you deposit money into a bank, say £10,000 - it's no longer, legally, your property. It is the bank's property, and because it no longer belongs to you, the banks are free to lend it out to whomever they so choose, at interest. They do not need your permission because it's no longer yours. Tough!

If you had left a gold candelabra with a friend and they had sold it and thus could not return it – that's theft under criminal law. Plain and simple. The banks can refuse to return your money. But that is a subject of civil law. It is not considered theft.

You deposited £10,000 of your fiat currency with a bank and in its place you have another piece of paper, a deposit slip - that guarantees - absolutely nothing! (It's only faith that attaches any value to either bit of paper)

If there was a 'run' on the bank – because there is a collapse of confidence in the bank, probably caused by the bankers lending too much money that did not exist, all their clients are left with are worthless pieces of paper.

You are not the legal owner of the money you deposited. That is why this arrangement exists. To protect the bankers. You have no recourse if your money goes south other than to sue. And that means suing a bank that has no means to pay – do you see the comparison in the reverse of this situation?

Chapter Six:
Banks Create Money from Thin Air

However, to protect the nation's commercial structure government will usually organise a bail-out to keep the economy afloat.

Why can't governments organise a bail-out if a private individual found they could not pay their creditors? Ho, ho, ho.

To continue the comparison.

If you deposited money in a bank, you have a receipt However, in that receipt, there was no schedule of tangible assets that the bank offered in exchange for your deposit of £10,000. Instead, you have a form of promissory note that promised nothing as the bank was under no legal obligation. If it has no funds. It can't pay, so it does not pay. It can go bust and you can't sue anybody. I don't think this was ever made clear on the paper they handed you.

If there is a run on the banks the banks lock their doors. The police can't be called to retrieve stolen property because it is not your property, it was not stolen, it was not a criminal act, it was gifted to the bank by a gullible, trusting member of the public - you.

The only time the police are summoned is if the crowd outside the bank becomes unruly, as they may well do. The police will break up any protest they consider out of hand even resorting to truncheons and water-cannon.

The police turn upon the victims of theft, not the perpetrators.

Most likely the government will bail out the bank with taxpayer's money. You are in effect paying taxes, that go to the bankers to reimburse the money that was yours in the first place.

Chapter Six:
Banks Create Money from Thin Air

The bankers may resign and often receive a fat severance, paid for by the very clients who they sought to rob.
The bankers win, and their clients and taxpayers lose
Sorry!

> *When a bank makes a loan, it simply adds to the borrower's deposit account in the bank by the amount of the loan. The money is not taken from anyone else's deposit; it was not previously paid into the bank by anyone. It's new money, created by the bank for the use of the borrower."* -
> *Robert B. Anderson, former US Secretary of the Treasury*

Remember this when we turn the tables and you walk away from the dept in chapter seven.

When you apply for a credit card or unsecured loan the bank asks you to sign a document, a virtual-promissory note, also known as a 'Security Document' or 'Security Instrument'.

Usually, these documents list tangible assets, such as bonds, stock, property, etc., that we pledged as security for the loan. We did not record any such assets - so is this document worth anything?

The receipt handed to you when you deposited £10,000 with the bank did not list tangible assets as a form of guarantee from the bank if it defaulted. It just recorded that you gave, yes gave, cash to the bank with no guarantee as to its return. Let's turn the tables.

Say your borrowing was for a limit of £5,000 on a credit card. The bank then enters this on a security document showing an agreed loan, or facility, up to the value of £5,000. This is then entered into a ledger as an asset of the bank. They have, via a piece of paper, created £5,000 - and they paid nothing for it.

Chapter Six:
Banks Create Money from Thin Air

What rights do the banks have to the money they fabricated from your debt that is now in your account?

When we stop paying, they will claim you had a binding agreement with them to repay. True you have the benefit of the money. But they could not have created that money if you did not request a loan – perhaps it was you that created the money for them from thin air and you owe them only the value of the said thin air?

Was it the same 'binding agreement' when we deposited £10,000 in cash at the bank and walked away with a piece of paper that we found later to be worth nothing?

If we ask for our money back that's the device by which the banks could legally refuse; there was no agreement for the bank to repay.

We argue if the contract between you and the bank for depositing money was fair when the contract states the bank is under no obligation to refund - and yet when the same bank deposits money with us, in the form of a loan, and we don't repay how can they say the contract with us is fair and binding when we compare both contracts side by side?

No court ought to enforce a contract which is contrary to public policy or to natural justice, which is illegal or immoral, or which is unconscionable or unfair.
Lord Wright. British Judge Ruling in 1966

This time it will be you who questions if they have a case to demand the return of any ghost money that went from their account to yours. A spurious argument, perhaps, but play with it in your replies and questions when we get to chapters seven and eight.

Chapter Six:
Banks Create Money from Thin Air

The 2008 banking crisis was based on trading in debt.

The 2008 crisis began with the collapse of the subprime mortgage market in the United States, where lenders gave loans to people who could not pay them back.

These loans were bundled together and sold as a debt folio. As housing prices began to fall, many borrowers found themselves with homes worth less than their mortgages. This led to a wave of foreclosures, which led to a decline in house prices and a significant loss of value for financial institutions that had invested (speculated) heavily in the mortgage market.

The crisis quickly spread beyond the US, affecting financial markets worldwide. Banks and other financial institutions had invested heavily in mortgage-backed securities, which were now worth far less than they had paid. This led to a credit freeze, as banks became reluctant to lend money to one another, causing a liquidity crisis.

The folio on debts that became a tradable commodity is commonly known as a "mortgage-backed security" (MBS). In other words, they traded in debts – like yours and mine. This securitisation process allowed banks and other financial institutions to package and sell large amounts of mortgage debt to investors worldwide – this has a bearing on the process we start in the next chapter.

For further discourse on banking fraud and scandals, go to chapter twelve at the end of this book

Chapter Seven

Debt Liberation Day

The first day forward - the liberation of your debt is delightfully simple.

The day your payment or payments are due – you don't.

A few weeks before you instructed your bank to cancel any direct debit associated with the account you want to be liberated from.

That was simple: Can't pay – then – don't pay.

No tears. No more payments. This month you put food on the table.

Chapter Seven
Debt Liberation Day

Wham! The heavens have not fallen in upon you. The SWAT team has not arrived. The SAS are not on your balcony.

I would not recommend doing this in North Korea, but otherwise, continue.

****

If you have more than one credit card, it's up to each credit card company to decide whether to continue with you.

I suggest defaulting on them all. If there is still a margin, you could take out the cash via an ATM, up to the limit, and keep the cash as a reserve. Battleground tactics—just this time.

Quite a decision, and your decision. But no more of an issue than defaulting on just one card.

If you decide to continue with the other cards, so be it. However, if they block you – don't pay, you no longer have an advantage in keeping that card - and follow the same course as the other cards.

Look at the story of my friend at the end of the book. He had about ten credit cards and was a total of £60,000 in debt when his ability to pay dried up.

Chapter Seven
Debt Liberation Day

First contact from the bank

Soon after your payment is missed you may receive an SMS informing you that your account is in arrears and thus blocked and (1) urge you to make a payment and (2) talk to their *'Overdue Account Collection Department on this telephone number?'*.

Gosh! Card blocked? – super, you don't want it anyway. Do not telephone them. They will record what you say and may use that against you. They are experienced in asking tricky questions, probably from a script, and that could fluster you. Take your time and only write in response to their letters. That also uses up a lot of their time.

Overdue Account Collection Department. Sounds official and scary; it's meant to be. And often this scary 'department" is not even located in the country you are resident and staffed by warlocks – ignore!

Within a week of your debt going unpaid - not delinquent yet – you will receive a stereotyped letter.

This tends to be of the type
"We assume you may have forgotten to make a payment. Please telephone to let us know how we can help."

What amazes me is that these letters have the same touching belief that they think we could even, for a second, believe they are sincere in wanting to '*help and understand.*'

For example:

These are the typical subheading in first first-response to a missed payment

"We can help you manage arrears on your account.",
"Please call us to discuss how we can help you." (Help you pay us),

Chapter Seven
Debt Liberation Day

"Managing your future payments… (for our benefit, not yours)
"Our next step if you don't get in touch." (Or else!).

The letter then goes on to tell you all the awful things they will do to you and how they really, really care about your situation – but on the other hand, pretty please, excuse the language, but not the sentiment:

"F***k you, pay me" (© the movie 'Wise Guys'.)

At this point realise several things about the banker's situation. You owe them money; you can't pay, proven because you have not paid. If they had a strong case against you, why not after the first few letters followed by a 'letter before action' (see later) whisk you off to court, get an order for you to pay, plus the legal costs and court fees and then throw you in a dungeon for daring to upset 'The Bank'?

Why threaten more than once? If they have a case that they were sure of winning, with full costs, against someone with the means to pay then they would take you to court with the minimum of correspondence.

From the movie 'The Good, the Bad and the Ugly."
"If you're going to shoot – shoot; don't talk."

They won't. They will wait it out until they hand your account over to a debt collection agency.

They know if they did win against someone who has no means to pay, how would they get paid? It's already clear that you don't have the ability to pay. It is a long, expensive and time-consuming journey from judgment to payment, with zero guarantees they will be successful.

They know judges will also consider the defendant's ability to pay and any extenuating circumstances and will probably reduce the award - if any. Plus, bankers almost certainly have

Chapter Seven
Debt Liberation Day

insurance that covers them for 'delinquent' accounts.
The time for them to receive insurance starts ticking away as soon as the first payment is missed. Why are they worried?

Bankers and debt collectors are in business to make money. If your case involves answering loads of questions that a junior member of staff can't reply to with certainty and hence can't reply with stereotyped letters. They will have to get out of their chair and involve expensive senior members of staff, or even their legal department - or even independent legal counsel. They will receive the advice to give up. They will be spending money, not making money if they have to answer all your questions, and they are obliged to answer all your questions if this is to go to court. So, the light at the end of the tunnel towards getting any money from you at a profit is getting dimmer.

Overall, financial institutions are profit-driven, and their primary concern is to ensure that their shareholders are adequately compensated.
As such, they tend to adopt pragmatic approaches to handling outstanding debts.

I repeat it is the tactic is to politely barrage them with loads of questions that by law demand answers – your letter will sit for a long time in their in-tray.

It is not that you will beat them with clever legal arguments, although you will present a fair few. It is because they will not bother to reply to questions. That is why it is not going to court. And when they have given up replying; they have given up chasing.

They will wait until they can sell your debt to a debt collection agency and be thankful to be rid of you.

Chapter Seven
Debt Liberation Day

Your letter

On their letter, they probably won't have a return address or at best a post office box number. A PO number is unusable as all your replies must be sent by recorded delivery. Search the internet for their registered office and address your letter for the attention of an executive officer. You should find their names listed on the company's registered site. It is a legal requirement. Then pick s name to target. From the account manager, if listed, to the CEO.

You will be turning the integration around in the politest way possible by asking *them* questions, loads of questions.

Take your time to formulate. I'll show you how.

Tell them repeatedly that you are 'struggling' to pay. Use whatever rhetoric but on no account say that you won't pay. Don't even indicate you can't pay. Then, technically, they have no grounds to take you to court, which is extremely unlikely in any event.

No judge or magistrate would be impressed by a bank or card company dragging a client before the court because they were 'struggling' to pay.

In other words, never acknowledge the debt. If you do, it could trigger two things – one: give ammunition to the satisfaction of the courts that an obligation exists, and two, acknowledgement of the debt resets the statute of limitations, (More on that later in chapter nine).

This is my recommendation:

Tell them you have been very distressed over this whole matter (say matter, never mention the word debt.) Then, give a short description of your situation, i.e., you have no funds available or disposable income, and you are, as said, struggling.

Chapter Seven
Debt Liberation Day

Now, this is a gem; tell them you have a friend with legal training (let's call her Margaret), and she is interested in your situation both as a friend and from a legal point of view. The idea of using a third person is to distance yourself from direct and personal confrontation. This works well. (We will cast her as a rather fussy lady with a panache for detail and who likes things in perfect and muddled order.)

With her help, you will ask difficult questions, such as the original agreement's true function, exact definitions, and obligations - if it still exists – the agreement that is.

This, to follow, is an oft-used, thus almost classic, retort when trying to trash the creditor's arguments; this time for the card company or bankers and next for the debt collection agency. It will be a thorn in the flesh for both of them. The point is we don't really want answers – just to use up their allocated time.
We want them to realise they have a pedantic pain in the butt to deal with, and they would rather close the book on the whole issue and move it on to a debt collection agency.

You tell them your friend has urged you to apply 'due diligence' (an excellent legal term), and you want to get off on the correct footing. Tell them we **both,** you and the bank, **need** to understand our relevant obligations.

Then say, like a child with a new toy, that it would be due diligence, keep repeating that, as your friend suggested, for you to answer the following:

The primary question tacitly attacks the assumption that they actually have any form of lien (or charge) or binding agreement over you.
Then we look at the agreement itself.

Chapter Seven
Debt Liberation Day

This is a little complex – all to the good - so a new sub-heading.

Your credit agreement – complexities arguments

A 'Security Instrument' or 'Security Document' is a tangible item that can and is traded, remember how in chapter six?

The agreement or contract, or whatever you signed with the bank, could also be called a 'security instrument' or 'security document. They are indeed legal documents whose purpose is to indicate what collateral or security you have pledged to the bank as the guarantee to repay a loan.
Yet the only guarantee is your signature.
Now if your signature on a paper, or electronic, is sufficient for the bank to file on their ledger as an asset and thus create money for a loan up to the maximum agreed, then that said agreement has the same intrinsic value. And that we will use in your argument.
Referencing this document's validity, possession and whereabouts, and who now owns it are a sample of the questions we will put to the bankers and debt agencies.

Claiming that the collateral equals the loan's agreed value is perhaps a spurious argument. However, we have a case enough when our debt was regarded by them as a tangible, tradable asset - enough value for them to create a loan and of enough value to any party willing to pay for it. It would be like a signed cheque left with them to cover the total amount of the loan.

But driving the point is that when we raise difficult questions about the status of our contract, they will be reluctant or unable to answer and begin to wish we would go away, bugger off - rather than be daunted by our clever legal rhetoric. Even if your argument is esoteric, flawed, and even creative, it does

Chapter Seven
Debt Liberation Day

not matter. What matters is they will have to spend time defending it – and that they will not be willing to do.

Many high court judges have gone to great lengths to clarify what different forms of contract mean, and they seem instead, to have made it more confusing.

If high court judges and top legal minds still debate this issue, and these issues are still put before the court on a regular basis, how well would the clerk at the bank, card company, or debt agency understand the legal implications well enough to reply to you directly without sending your questions up a floor or two – they won't.

Another point that invites scrutiny, and you will scrutinise every aspect, is that the agreement with the bankers _"may be updated or amended occasionally."_ What? Can we, as the consumer, also unilaterally amend the agreement? Something is not quite right here. Worth interrogation and more questions? Absolutely!

Also, bear in mind you can say something not quite correct in your correspondence and excuse yourself for the mistake because you misunderstood and are a layperson. Much harder for the banks, card companies and agencies, all professionals, to fall back on the same excuse if it ever came before a judge – and going to court is very unlikely to happen.

Also, if professional lawyers become involved and are asked to give an opinion on a worthless debt, they will be aware of either the ruling by Lord Justice Clarke, a British judge who served as a Lord Justice of Appeal in 2002, or the sentiment and legal implications it elicits as other countries also have strict disciplines and understanding and abide by the stringent rules of law.

Chapter Seven
Debt Liberation Day

I quote:

"Failure by the lender to observe strictly the intricate requirement of the Act can lead to the loan being completely unenforceable with no rights of restitution or other forms of relief"
Lord Justice Clarke

So, do they add the risk of a mistake, or cock-up, by junior clerks to a flimsy action against a worthless debt? I don't think so.

Chapter Seven
Debt Liberation Day

You will ask them to provide a copy of the security document, contract, agreement or whatever they want to call it whereby they have alleged a debt.

Wham!

And, exercising due diligence, you would like to have this checked over.

Also, you read somewhere that banks can unilaterally amend agreements. You need to know if there are any amendments, additions, or subtractions to the said 'agreement' you may not be aware of since you purportedly signed. If so, may you have full details of how the original alleged agreement was altered from the first time you started using my card?

Further, ask if the agreement would be physically returned to you if the debt is not proven, or do they intend to keep it as a debt, an asset, in a portfolio, and file it as an acquisition of the banks, with your name, or do they intend to sell on to whatever derivative market that currently exists, or they intend to create?

And that you are sorry for all the questions; it's just that you want to understand everything and apply due diligence.

Space these questions out over several letters in reply.

Do you remember the detective series Columbo on television? Use his tactic. Write a load of bumph that needs, by law, a response, then at the very end

"*Oh, just another thing I thought I should ask ...*" and then come in with a spurious yet painfully pedantic question.

Chapter Seven
Debt Liberation Day

Your first letter

This is a suggested draft letter crystalizing the above points

Mr John Smith
Account manager
ABC Credit Card Company
Company House

(They have your address for return correspondence, but add it again if you like.)

Your reference 123456

Sent via recorded delivery dated __ __ ____

Dear Mr John Smith,

Thank you for your letter of the (date)
I have a good friend, who is advising me and she has asked me to exercise 'due diligence'; I hope that's okay?
She asked that I put to you the following questions, and requests, in response to your letter:

She advised that I should have a copy of the original agreement.

Chapter Seven
Debt Liberation Day

She has also advised me that the bank, your good selves, can unilaterally amend and change the rules of this agreement.

Could you please let me have copies of all subsequent revisions and amendments pertaining to and leading up to your request for payment? I don't think I have one, or any, or indeed if I have ever received a copy.

It is called a Security

She would like to check the agreement's terms and our joint liabilities, responsibilities and obligations, she advised me that the bank has a legal responsibility to provide the answers to these requests and questions - as above - and to follow.

One thing that I find disturbing is that when I allegedly signed the security document you created this money from nothing and entered this as a debt on your ledger. I quote:

" When banks lend, they create money out of thin air. The money supply is not fixed; it is created afresh by banks when they lend." The Financial Times

This can't be true – I am incredulous can you advise the validity, or otherwise, of that statement?

You see, from that I can only deduce that this document has value so can you explain what you intend to do with it once this matter is resolved – do you intend to return it to me or will you be selling it to a third party?

I look forward to your reply whereupon my friend will read and advise and I will get back to you as soon as possible

Chapter Seven
Debt Liberation Day

> Yours sincerely
> With respect.
> Pain in the butt

Keep the letter simple and the requests difficult.

Once sent do not worry if you don't get an immediate reply or any reply. That is to your advantage. *If* this ever went to court then the judge would not be too impressed when you show the receipts for letters sent that were not answered. Make sure you file all letters clearly with the posting receipt. If you get a copy of the agreement, take it to bits line by line. Ask them to 'confirm or deny' every part you are unhappy about and even parts you are happy about.

The object is to use up their allocated time so they will leave you alone.
Then ask. "There are other things I have always been worried about with my account…choose a point at random saying "I would appreciate your reply and some explanations as to the merit, or otherwise, of these issues."

They will probably ignore your request. You can then expect them to go silent for some time. Always be polite but firm.

In a subsequent reply, or maybe in your first letter, choose your timing, and slip in this question:

It will rattle them.

> "As I understand from my friend, and sadly, the implicit threats, you may be handing this matter over to a Debt Collection Agency.
> That sounds terrible. I think it is outrageous.
> Please can you confirm that the ABC Credit Card Company has adequately vetted this agency and that

Chapter Seven
Debt Liberation Day

you have used due diligence and investigated the ethical handling of any disputes, past and present, and assure me they will not be harassing me or in any way be breaking the law?

I hear these agencies have a fearsome reputation, and your sincere assurances would be so much appreciated."

The bank or card company realise they will be in a difficult situation if they told you they vetted the company - or claim that it was not their responsibility - if later you are forced to issue a 'Cease & Desist' order. (More on that later in the next chapter.)

That allows you to threaten to bring a formal complaint, or counterclaim, of illegal misconduct or harassment against the agency and, of course, implicating the bank. Drop hints to this effect in any ensuing letter they have not satisfactorily replied to - and use this opportunity as a possible segue into using the 'dirty hands' legal phrase – see later.

If you ever bought such an action and produced the above letter as evidence in court, the best for them would be an embarrassment – the worst, a legal and expensive, reprimand.

Of course, you never intend to go to court – you are continuing the bluff. And doing it very well.

Always avoid answering direct questions.
When, or if, they start asking questions. Then, take a break and watch an expert on not answering questions—only about 90 seconds. This is genuinely amusing. Well worth watching.

Michael Howard, the British politician, cabinet member and leader of the conservative party, was asked the same question by Jeremy Paxman, the interviewer, 12 times in 90 seconds. Each time, dear Michael avoided an answer.

Chapter Seven
Debt Liberation Day

A lesson on how to avoid questions you dont want to answer

A true expert, even as a politician, in not answering a direct question.
So, if you are asked directly about your debt and do not want to reply, do a 'Michael Howard' and loop, dive and obfuscate until they stop asking.

Check out the QR or click if you are reading on a PC/tablet. "Demanding an Answer: Jeremy Paxman v Michael Howard'

For example, your reply to each question should be something like this. And always apologise for doing so.

"The question should not be that, it should be this." sort of retort.
Example:
"The question is not what I can afford to pay but how can I afford to pay, and why should I pay?".
An excellent turnaround that there is no answer they can submit, and you are the one now asking questions

Q. "How did you get in debt?"
A. "How could I not go into debt with the current situation?"
Q. "You have an obligation under law to pay, do you agree?"
A. "Yes, but how can I agree if I don't know what I am agreeing to? Please may I have a copy of the agreement you refer to? My friend urges due diligence and has asked me to obtain this for her to check."

Chapter Seven
Debt Liberation Day

Then, as said, if they send you the agreement (unlikely), go through it line by line, picking, probing, and asking all sorts of questions.

And so on.

The bankers or card companies will be easy to deal with as they have little to lose. They are biding time until they get insurance, or if they have assumed the risk and the algorithm kicks in, to sell the debt and walk away.

Use the same tactics for the debt collection agency in the next chapter. They have far less power, and you are well protected under the law from harassment, but as theirs is a 'grab what they can by any means' philosophy - they will be far more tenacious.

Back to the bankers and credit card people:
Each time they receive a question, they have a legal obligation to compose an answer in reply. Each time another letter, and each time a few more weeks go by.
They will eventually stop asking, as the interviewer, Jeromy Paxman, out of exasperation, did.

Another quote from H. White, the chairman of the New Zealand Monetary Commission.
"Banks do create money. They have been doing it for a long time...you will find it in all sorts of documents and textbooks...I doubt very much if you would get a prominent banker to deny this."

What if the bank or agency asks you to complete a 'financial audit'?

If they ask for information about your current financial status, you are not legally required to provide them with information. Only a court can order that.

Chapter Seven
Debt Liberation Day

They will still try and usually provide you with a legal-looking and horribly foreboding form, probably with a grey border, asking for all personal details – how much you spend on food, drink, cigarettes, telephone, clothing, and how much you owe other people, friends and family, and so on.

Your response can be a double-edged sword.

<u>You are reasonably entitled to refuse.</u>

You can politely decline to give this information, stating that a 'strip search' of your finances is an invasion of your privacy, something you are naturally sensitive about and adding immensely to your distress and emotional state and fear of derision and harassment.

State quite clearly that you understand that they have no legal right to insist on this, and you hope they, in return, understand why you chose to decline.

Suppose they have not advised you that this is, in fact, not a legal requirement, document, or obligation they can enforce but has been presented to you portending it was. In that case, you will seek some form of remedy by a matter of formal complaint at a later date. (A good counter-threat if they continue to pursue.)

If the requests become persistent or are accompanied by any threat, then you have the right to claim their actions as harassment – something they, in turn, would be very sensitive about.

It should be sufficient for their records to state that you are in a situation where you are struggling (repeat, don't say struggling <u>to pay debts</u>, but just struggling.) and have, in any event, no disposable income.

Chapter Seven
Debt Liberation Day

Also, be aware that if you do submit to completing this form, any information proven to be proven <u>deliberately</u> inaccurate or misleading can be seen as fraud. Thus, a criminal act, rather than a civil action, could be used against you by the courts. Unlikely, but possible, keep that in mind.

On the other hand, completing this form shows the banks or debt collectors that you really do not have sufficient income to meet your debts.

It would be like puncturing their balloon. They would have nothing to pursue you for – they would, with any sense, see no further point in chasing this claim.

Adios mi amigos.

Depending on how you feel, both courses of action have their merits. My preference is the first option. It's like a game of chess. See what their next move is.

After about three months, with probably more letters that you field with more questions, is for the bankers or card company to tell you they have "handed the matter over" or 'assigned

Chapter Seven
Debt Liberation Day

the matter' – a much nicer term - to their 'debt collection department'.
That's usually garbage!

In most cases, they have auctioned your debt to a debt collection agency for a few percent of the original balance Debt collection agencies often purchase large portfolios of debts from multiple creditors, which allows them to spread their risk and increase their chances of making a profit.

They may have instead retained or contracted the agency to collect on their behalf – very rare - but a little more complicated. Use the same tactics, but they will be more persistent. Not necessarily more effective, but more persistent.

The specialist agency would want repeat business with the banks and will try their best to get results. This is only likely to happen if a) there is a substantial debt owing and b) the debtor has a property or other assets they suspected to be hiding that can be tracked and attacked. Leading ultimately to an embargo placed by a court. (Depending on the country.)

Another legal saying is, *"Do not sue a man of straw."* Good advice. Convince them you are made of straw, lots of it. Well, at least your current bank balance is straw; you are certainly not.

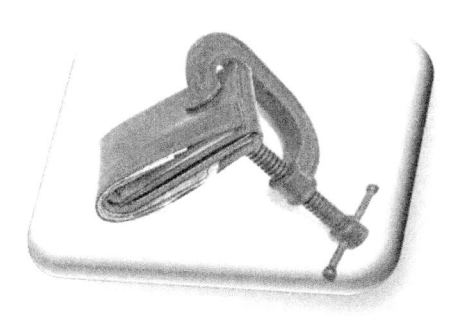

Chapter Eight

The debt collection agency

> *"Debt collectors have become the face of the debt industry, and unfortunately, the face of the debt industry is not a friendly one."* - Robert Manning, author of *"Credit Card Nation: The Consequences of America's Addiction to Credit"*

Don't panic.
Seriously step back and think about this for a moment. If the banks thought they could win in court, they would take you to court! No further discussion. Instead, they sold your dept for a few cents on the dollar. They gave up chasing; they believed the debt was almost worthless.

It is. You have won the first phase.
The bankers and card people will no longer chase you.

Now it is the debt collection agency's turn to chance its arm, using whatever tactics it can devise to get back more than it paid.

However, as discussed, there is a caveat: be aware the agency will come in one of two manifestations:
Either via the original creditor, the bank or credit card company has instructed or hired the agency to collect the debt on their behalf They are acting as an agent on behalf of the bankers attempting to recover the debt for a fee. The bankers still own the debt via the security instrument and are ultimately responsible for any legal action against you, not the agency.

Chapter Eight
The debt collection agency

Or - very much more likely - the debt has been sold outright to the debt collection agency. They now claim to be the debt's legal 'owner' and scrabble to get whatever they can.

The first letter from the agency

We have the first letter or perhaps email. Remember, it´s all bluster and bluff.
It will be similar to the one you received from the bank or card company.
Usually with a *"Remember, we are here to help you work out a payment schedule - or else"* sub-heading, mingled with threat, quoting all sorts of consumer laws and sub-sections to make it look more daunting.
You will not be daunted.
You are going to use a repeat of the letter you used for the banks with just a few extra questions interrogating what rights they have assumed by contacting you directly.

The bank may have already informed you that they are handing this over to a debt collection agency, or may even refer to it as 'their' debt collection department – no matter what, ask the agency again in your first letter, explaining also that you are applying 'due diligence' to this matter and you do not recognise there is an outstanding debt - and let them take time to respond.

Next, ask the agency to provide information about the status of your alleged debt. Are they working on behalf of the original creditor, or have they purchased the alleged debt and are now acting on their own initiative?

Whatever the scenario, could they please send copies of the contract between you and the bankers or credit card company and between the debt agency and the instructing party or the party that sold the debt so you know where you stand?

Chapter Eight
The debt collection agency

Even ask them, continuing with the utmost respect of course, how much they paid for the alleged debt as you think it is pertinent for you to know (it is not pertinent, of course – well, not at this stage - see later in the section on credit rating reference a 'pay-for-delete agreement').

They will probably refuse to answer – but it's fun to ask. Remember, as with the bankers, you have never acknowledged the dept and only said, if you say anything at all, is that you were 'struggling'. You have not even said what you were struggling with.

The reason is that in most countries if you don't **refute the debt within 30 days in writing**, the debt is considered valid in law. You plan to challenge anyway but keep well within this time frame. And always send via recorded delivery

Once you dispute the debt, they can't contact you further until they have provided sufficient verification of the debt in writing.

'Sufficient verification' is a wonderful term. Almost like 'beyond reasonable doubt'. Play on that theme.

Again, as suggested in the last section, you claim that you have a friend with legal training who is helping you and has urged you to apply 'due diligence as you have already mentioned. You want to get off on the correct footing; hence you need to understand their function and motive.

You will also need to find their correspondence address from the Internet - and the names of the directors – so you may send letters by recorded delivery.

Adopt the same procedure as when dealing with bankers and card companies but be more persistent in interrogating what proof of the alleged debt they actually hold. From experience, it is rare indeed that they can produce any proof whatsoever.

Chapter Eight
The debt collection agency

Repeatedly ask what sort of contract exists between you and the agency, not between the agency and the bank, but this time between you and the agency, as they seem to assume powers you don't recognise. By what authority do they pursue for a debt you have not acknowledged?
Juggle the phrasing to suit the tone of the letter you are replying to.

In a tacit way query their anticipated outcome in prosecuting this alleged debt. What do they expect? Because whatever happens, this is a debt you have no means to pay.

They will dislike dealing with this and spending time to answer – so be it.
Stay polite.

Continue as you did with the bank – pedantic, persistent and a pain in the arse.

Even get on first-name terms if they have a consistent agency employee who regularly contacts you. But, then, just let it drop now and again, tacitly and in the best possible taste, that they have no hope in hell of ever getting a single penny out of you.

Debt-collecting firms have a well-deserved bad reputation. They are the scavengers of the legal world, the carpet baggers, opportunists, the pariahs, and parasites by the exact definition. They are like vultures seeing if there is anything left over after the others gave up on you.

However much the threats, bluster and rhetoric, they have little power. They have paid peanuts for your debt; anything they can get over and above is pure profit.

Their tactic is to bully and harass until they get some cash from a stressed and scared individual. So be disciplined and

Chapter Eight
The debt collection agency

polite in your replies. Edge away from being sarcastic. Sarcasm in any dealings only antagonizes. You are actually in a stronger position than they are. They know it. They don't want to go to court, but they will try to convince you they do.

Don't panic – yes, I know at first it's scary – stand firm. I repeat they have very little to stand on legally. Remember, most of the letters will be stereotyped, and a computer will make most of the decisions based on a clerk checking yes-no boxes – but at some time, a human will intervene and have to decide whether to take court action.

Very unlikely, but, as with the banks, if you upset or insult a human, they may become vindictive and seek private revenge. In other words, if the banter has become unpleasant, or they see you as a smart-arse or crook, that might swing the decision - if the decision is on the cusp - to go for litigation.

Meantime they will be skirting the very edge of the law and even stepping over it – with very little in the way of actual power. They rely on fear, your vulnerability and their perception of your ignorance concerning the law.

Your tactic is to waste so much of their senior staff or legal adviser's time, that they will give up. When you start probing and asking questions, they have to spend time drafting itemised letters, researching and presenting documents, and they will take the view that "This is not worth it".

Continue showing that you are neither scared of them nor ignorant of the law - nor a smart-ass. The bankers did not want to take you to court. If they reasonably expected to win in court, why would they waste all that time on you? The same motivation will be uppermost with the agency – but they will try to bully you!

Chapter Eight
The debt collection agency

Similar to bankers, the agencies are pragmatic. So, convince them they will have to expend energy, loads of work, time and money producing documents and answering questions - that by law, they should, but in practice, they probably can't or won't.

If they purchased the debt from the bank for a percentage of the principal amount and are then faced with a barrage of questions followed by the dawning realisation that you know the game they are playing and that you have no intention of paying, or more truthfully, you convince them you have no means of paying – they will weigh up the situation, or their AI bots or whatever algorithms they use – the most likely scenario is they, will give up.

It will be slightly more challenging if the banks have retained the agency on their behalf because they believe you have some assets, but the same tactics apply – make it not worth their while to continue.

Yes, there is a chance, a very slight chance, that they will elect to take you to court. But, at this stage, they are a long, long way from ever doing that.

As with the banks avoid phone conversations! They have tricks that you may not have time to respond to, and they record what you say. They are practised in intimidation and work to the very edge of the law.

They have far more experience in this field than you. It depends on your location, but most districts and countries forbid agencies from contacting you by phone without your permission.

So, don't give your permission.

Chapter Eight
The debt collection agency

If they try phoning, make sure you have their name logged into your contacts so it shows on your phone when they call again. If they use multiple phone numbers and you pick up because you didn't recognize the number, say, "Sorry. I´m hard of hearing and don't understand what's being said; who am I speaking to anyway? Sorry, I didn't hear that - is that the pizza takeaway?" - that sort of thing.

One chap I interviewed told me he feigned an asthma attack while on the phone with the agency. He gasped it was because of all the stress and then hung up. He never heard another word from them.
It was true, he was stressed, and he did suffer from asthma but this time he faked it. That was over six years ago - the statute of limitations had passed.

Wouldn´t it be wonderful to divert their calls to a call centre in Bangladesh with the staff reading back to them from a script you prepared? That's after a 15-minute wait with loads of irritating music.
You could, of course, if we reach the stage of the agency repeatedly telephoning have some canned music ready. Then if you do get a call - say, "Sorry" (or rather – "sorreeeeeeee!") then; "got - to - put - you - on - hold – for - a few - minuteeeees. Another call coming eeeen.")
Then bugger off for a few hours.

Seriously if you feel they are harassing you either from their tone, threats, tacit or explicit or bombarding you with letters, phoning when they shouldn't, sending multiple emails and so on. If you are harassed in this way, send another letter also by recorded delivery. Start with

Chapter Eight
The debt collection agency

brief details of your grievance, then in bold type on a separate line, add that you want them to;

**"Cease & Desist with Immediate Effect!
I have nothing more to add."**

It will have an impact and shake them up. Scary stuff - for them this time.

Of course, a 'cease & desist.' issued other than by court is a request - a stern warning that you will take this matter further. All bluff. But good bluff, because it shows you mean business.

When a court issues that exact term, it becomes an order. Failure to comply could lead to a 'contempt of court' notice— a serious and expensive matter.

Also, if this did come to court and it was read out before the court that the agency received a *'Cease & Desist'* request – and they ignored it - you could have scored some points in your favour with the judge. And the agency knows that. But this is not going to court.

The tone of their subsequent correspondence may start to harden as time passes and they get more desperate. Make sure your questions about your account will need personal attention – and, in all probability, it will never come. (They did say they were there to 'help you sort out your finances' – translate that however you will but helping you is not on the agender)

Keep pushing them to take a realistic approach. The line of least resistance. Their decision is driven by economic considerations, such as the cost-effectiveness of pursuing the debt in court and the insurance coverage available for such risks.

Chapter Eight
The debt collection agency

Make the agency aware of your financial situation - you cannot pay – already tested by the bankers – continue to interrogate and stipulate your legal rights, supported by due diligence from a legal, pedantic friend.

You will achieve a stalemate – then you are the winner

Don't worry; they're all bluffs, threats and bluster. That's about all they have. Be aware that their only path is to scare you into submission; they will push that to the limit

1) They will attempt intimidation – it does not work because you will not be intimidated.

2) They will attempt to make you feel shame – it does not work because the shame is on them and the bankers, not you.

3) They will come as close to harassment as possible – it does not work because the law is very much on your side in this respect.

Stick it out, don't worry and follow my advice – they have very little else to use when you counter those three shameful tactics.

Letter Before Action

However, let's explore the scenario that they have 'upped the ante', and double-bluffed that they intend to take you to court, or rather, they threaten and scare you into believing they plan to go to court they are then legally obliged to send you a 'letter before action'. This, as said, is unlikely and thus hypothetical, but worth reading and noting.

A 'letter before action' is a formal letter sent by the plaintiff to the defendant before they can start legal proceedings to recover the alleged debt.

It must make clear they are the creditor. They must have

Chapter Eight
The debt collection agency

sufficient proof that they are. (You have not acknowledged any of this.) They must state the amount owed and the reason for the action.

From research, the law in most jurisdictions and countries states the letter must include the following requirements (listed below.) Failing to follow this means, in the improbable event it got this far, you could have the matter thrown out on a technicality.

1. Details of the debt: The letter should clearly state the amount of the debt owed, the name of the original creditor, and the date the debt was incurred.

2. Payment request: The letter should request that the debtor pays the debt in full within a specified period, usually 14 days.

3. Consequences of non-payment: The letter should clearly state that legal proceedings will be started if the debt is not paid within the specified time. It should also explain the potential consequences of this, such as additional costs and interest.

4. Information on debt advice: The letter should provide information on where the debtor can seek debt advice and support, such as from a debt advice charity.

5. Contact details: The letter should provide contact details for the creditor so that the debtor can get in touch if they have any questions or concerns.

If there are errors or omissions, even in the slightest detail you can reject it – in writing by recorded delivery - pointing out their error(s)

Chapter Eight
The debt collection agency

Dear Sirs,

I reject your letter before action as it has the following errors or omissions. If this ever becomes before a court, I will make them fully aware.

(Then go on to list any errors, or make them up, it does not matter how random. Frustrate them, thus stalling and further encouraging them to abort the claim.)

Please be aware, therefore, that your 'letter before action' is null and void – until, or unless, I hear from you again. Yours sincerely.

The clincher, the best tactic – if the arguments over the 'Letter Before Action' are used up – or maybe during - is to ask the following:

"Could you please provide me with copies of all the papers, documents, correspondence, and drafts of all the emails between us (with the names of the authors of these said documents*) that you intend to put before the court in pursuance of your claim?"

*If you have received a letter or email without the <u>name of the person</u> who wrote it and their signature, or without the current date, that will give you a good argument to refute as it's not a viable or legal communication.

Suddenly the plaintiffs (the debt agency) are faced with the enormous job of copying documents they may not be in possession of or having to contact the bank or card company for the same, which, as they have washed their hands of the matter, may not be that willing to put in extra time and effort to provide at probably short notice.

All for a trial that may never come pursuing a bad debt they are unlikely to obtain, even risking the judgment going against them. There is always a chance a judge or magistrate may be

Chapter Eight
The debt collection agency

more sympathetic to the defendant and least to a debt collection agency, particularly if there is even a hint of harassment.

In legal terms, the requested furnishing of documents from either side is called 'discovery'.

The agency with any business sense will evaluate this request they are legally obliged to furnish. Will they go ahead with all the work and expense to seriously attempt to sue to gain a doubtful payment from a defendant who has already proved they are struggling? The bankers or card companies had already given up on the defendant. They had washed their hands by selling the debt for peanuts. The costs before litigation were the few percent they paid for the debt. Would they proceed and take the risk and engage expensive lawyers to argue the claim in court?

Depending on the country, the legal fees are usually capped. So even if they won the case against a defendant without assets, their legal fees could exceed what the court was prepared to award, leaving the plaintiff paying the difference between what the lawyers billed and what the judge allowed.

Suing would not be good business. The agency would make no money because the salient fact is even if they won the total claimed plus expenses they are still in the same position – they have a debtor who can't pay.

So, their only tactic is to bluff about court action hoping it will intimidate you.

Call their bluff and stand firm.

And then, if - a big if - *if* you actually receive said copies of the documents, you can go over them with a fine tooth-comb and ask further questions, and more questions that they have

Chapter Eight
The debt collection agency

to answer, and then somewhere in your correspondence drop hints that you may be seeking to file for bankruptcy as you see no other choice.

Considering all the above, the chances of this ever going to court are minimal.

Language and clarity

While researching, I came up with some interesting facts.

A contract between parties must be seen as fair, transparent and <u>understood by both sides.</u>

<u>A</u>round 270,000 British citizens permanently live in the EU. Most of these guys would need local bank accounts. From my experience, banks do not always offer their contracts in a language other than that of the county they are resident.

A foreign language is challenging in small print and with legal jargon.

How many British, German, Spanish, or French sign a contract without understanding? How can it be said that both parties understood and thus can make a judgement as to the transparency and fairness of the contract? As far as they knew, they could by agreeing to be sent to a penal colony on Anthrax Island if they defaulted.

The interpretation of this rule will depend on the jurisdiction and the country, the mood of the judge, and precedent if any.

I relate this from experience; a friend recently had the threat of court action over a business deal rescinded. He signed a contract written in a language he did not understand. His solicitor pointed this out to the plaintiff and threatened to use that in court - the action was dropped. They agreed on an alternative solution.

Chapter Eight
The debt collection agency

You may have signed a credit agreement on a contract in a language you may not be fluent enough to understand. Worth pointing this out if you are now dealing with a debt-collecting agency. Phrase your question to elicit a non-ambiguous reply.

"Can you confirm or deny that the law of contract states that a written agreement between parties must be seen to be fair, transparent and understood by both sides?
How, then, can you say this contract is now enforceable when I did not understand the language it was written sufficiently enough to understand? I was coerced into signing by the clerk as he indicated a 'pressure of time' by looking at me, then the contract while tapping his watch."

It takes a lot of skill and knowledge for them to bring legal action correctly. Any error, even a minor one, can be amplified on interrogation and used to scupper their claim.

Failure by the lender to observe strictly the intricate requirement of the Act can lead to the loan being completely unenforceable with no rights of restitution or other forms of relief.
Lord Justice Clarke

You win. Well done. You are free. Start living again.

Credit Rating Agencies

> *"Credit rating agencies are supposed to provide an independent evaluation of creditworthiness, but in practice, they have become a key player in the financial industry, promoting the interests of issuers and investors over those of the general public."*
> Jack Reed, US Senator

Credit rating agencies compile your credit score by analysing your credit history. the amount of debt you owe, the length of your credit history, the types of credit you have, and the number of new credit applications you have submitted recently – and, of course, if you have defaulted or have been overdue too often. This is churned over by a computer to give you a score. Hence, different agencies will interpret the score differently depending on the algorithm.

As you already appreciate, your credit rating will be hit pretty badly. At the time you jailbroke your debt you may have chosen between eating or paying so there was not much else you could have done – apart from going hungry.

Your 'score' will improve over the years but can be a hassle. Get over it. If you want a mobile phone on contract – use pay-as-you-go.

Another credit card – don't! use debit cards.

A mortgage – get another family member to buy.

A new car on credit leasing – don't! Get a second-hand car you can afford.

Renting: landlords may want a considerable deposit - try negotiating - a hassle but doable.

Do not seek debt. Don't let debts seek you – interest payments are another cost of living. If you can't afford to buy - you can't afford the added cost of credit.

Credit Rating Agencies

In the meantime – to hell with your credit rating, you do not need 'good merit' marks as you did at school.
I recommend a few books at the end of this one on debt management.

Bankers supply information to credit rating bureaus for the end benefit of the banks.
Banks thus control the information; forming a perfect symbiosis for them and an imperfect distribution of facts for the people.
Similar to a police force who are employed to follow the rules of government, and are thus controlled by government.
C.V.J.

Be aware if you were taken to court and you agreed to pay over time - you would still have a negative report on your credit rating! That's the way it works. No kindness there. So not paying has at least preserved some capital
Time is one factor in improving your credit score. After the statute of limitations has passed your old debt should be expunged.
You could, if you came into an inheritance, a better job, or won the lottery, seek a 'Pay for Delete' agreement. This also reinforces the adage that you can only get credit when you prove you don't need it.
I don't recommend this approach.
Another suggestion to improve your credit rating and some debt agencies actually suggest this, is to get whatever credit cards you can – they are available. You will be whacked with some hefty fees and interest rates.
When you get the card, use it, and never exceed what you can't pay back at the end of the month. Then, do the same the following month.
Then seek out another card company same procedure.
Never going into debt.

Credit Rating Agencies

Depending on the way banks report to credit rating agencies your credit rating should improve.

My advice: if you have got this far don't get into a situation where you need to borrow again.

Check out the books at the end. Sure, not fun to miss the best things in life because you can't afford them.

The real value of money is not the trinkets you can buy but freedom of choice.
C.V.J.

The purpose of this book - to keep it simple – was to get you to get out of your current debt. I hope I have.

Dealing with credit rating agencies and your credit score is not within the ambit of this book.
While researching the field of Credit Collection Agencies I was sinking deeper into the murky parallel worlds of banking, money fabrication, swindles, debt creation and debt reporting agencies. Who are the masters of these worlds – who are the slaves?

Debt reporting agencies warrant a book on its own so I am researching a sequel investigating the suffocating big brother that dictates your economic/social standing - your credit score - and how to improve and possibly circumvent it.

An industry dealing in personal and erstwhile private information for the banker's benefit, garnered from information supplied by the bankers, an industry worth an estimated $20 billion a year - is going to be very defensive.

Credit Rating Agencies

Both the industry itself, and those that report, or have written about it, generate more hogwash and lies than can be contained in a few pages.

I will sort the wheat from the chaff. I will investigate who started it. Who really controls them? How much influence do the bankers, directly or indirectly have on the way reports are presented, collated, analysed and published? I will seek out corruption and bribes and I will seek ways to counter the damage done by the draconian theft of your dignity.

If you are interested in a specially discounted launch offer for the paperback or a free Kindle version that I will hold open for the first 10 days, send me an email.

Charles@literarycat.org

No message is needed, although I am happy to receive one, just in the subject line write "Reporting Agencies. Your new book"

I will send an email as soon as they are available

I promise I will not abuse your trust or sell your email address to a third party.

Chapter Nine

Statute of Limitations

AKA - Statute Barred or Prescribed

Probably after the dust has settled, you will not hear anything from the debt collection agency for a long time - if ever. You called their bluff – ignored their threats and blustering. Hopefully, now just silence. Your debt has disappeared forever.

The period from the default to the last date a summons can be issued is the 'Statute of Limitations'. Details with broad brush strokes are below, noting that the timing and conditions will vary in the EU from country to country and in the USA from state to state.

It is important to note that the information provided is a general overview of the Statute of Limitations. Check on the internet for whatever country or state you live in and the laws that apply. Just be aware there is certainly a time limit applied to the debt, after which, and under conditions similar to those listed, your debt will no longer be enforceable.

If the agency applies for court action before the statute has expired, the statute restarts at point zero. That would be very unlikely if the account laid dormant for some time unless, equally unlikely, new information has come to light.

The Statute of Limitations is six years in England and Northern Ireland and five years in Scotland.

If the creditor waits too long in Scotland, the debt will become known as 'prescribed'—a different name for the

Chapter Nine
Statute of Limitations

same process. Similarly, once a debt is prescribed, the law says it no longer exists, so there's nothing more the creditor can do to collect it.

In the United States, it is seven years.

The countdown typically begins from the first delinquency or missed payment date.

After this period, provided it is not resurrected by any of the conditions listed in the next section, your debt will become 'Statute Barred`. Meaning it can no longer be recovered through court action. This effectively means the debt is written off in real-world terms, never again to see the light of day, even though, in legal terms, it still exists.
You have not cleared the debt - it has just become unenforceable.

Make a note of the date in your diary. Then, hold a party and rejoice.

So, to recap, even though you still owe the debt (unless formally written off by the bank or card company – very, very unlikely – they will go silent), there is now very little, if anything, they can do if the time limit is exceeded.

The statute usually starts after the following:

a) The last signed letter from you

b) The last time you wrote to the creditor acknowledging that you owed the debt, i.e., a signed letter from you to the creditor. In some cases, an email can also count as written acknowledgement.

c) Regarding acknowledging a debt, don't! Keep to the format 'that you are struggling'. You are not even

Chapter Nine
Statute of Limitations

struggling to pay, just struggling. Be careful with the language used, and do not provide any information that could be used against you. Keeping track of any communication regarding the debt and when you made the last payment is also essential.

Leave the 'struggling' comment as vague as possible, and obfuscate your intentions regarding payment – or rather - no payment.

d) The last time you made a payment to the debt

e) The earliest date the creditor could have started court action.

The following do not count as a written acknowledgement of a debt:

1) A letter from you to the creditor clearly stating you don't owe the debt

2) A letter from the creditor to you

3) Speaking to a creditor over the phone

Depending on the law in different countries, if a creditor has already started court action before the end of the limitation period, none of the above applies– the debt will never become statute-barred or prescribed while a court action is pending.

Even as the statute becomes close to expiry, the courts don't like last-minute actions. They will take a negative view against the plaintiffs, particularly a debt collection agency, both for their tardiness and the extra burden of work they have caused the court via their delay.

The courts also don't consider it fair for a creditor to wait many years to take action when vital paperwork could have

Chapter Nine
Statute of Limitations

been lost, or a very old debt; the details and counterarguments forgotten. The debt collection agencies also know this and will probably back off any last-ditch attempt as it could be expensive and maybe pointless, profitless litigation for them.

In a nutshell.
What we have covered so far.

Stop paying
When letters arrive, reply. Be polite, say you are struggling, but never acknowledge the debt.
'Michael Howard' any questions they ask – befuddle them.
Waste their time until they give up.
By asking as many pedantic questions that require detailed answers.
Ditto the same procedure with the debt agency.
Wait for the end of the statute.
Wave goodbye to your current debt.

Chapter Ten

Bankers & Robbers

Banks Cheating on Their Customers.

To follow is not essential reading; hence I have placed it at the end of the book - but I still interesting reading.

> *"Banking scandals are a symptom of a larger problem: the deregulation and lack of oversight that has allowed banks to become too big to fail, too big to jail, and too big to care about their customers."*
> *Matt Taibbi*
> *Matt Taibbi gained widespread recognition for his coverage of the 2008 financial crisis. His reporting on the actions of Wall Street firms and the government's response to the crisis earned him a National Magazine Award nomination in 2009.*

Chapter Ten
Bankers & Robbers

Banks are buildings and institutions, often grand buildings of marble and granite, built to impress, dominate, and emanate wealth, stability and security (of course, paid for by their customers.)
Sure, the hardworking clerks at the counter probably have no idea of the schemes being cooked up by the guys on the top floors.
And not all bankers should be tarred with the same brush. But those honest bankers remain remarkably quiet or perhaps don't have an interesting enough media image while their industry is at an apogee, the lowest level, of respect and public confidence.

What do we call those who scheme, create money from nothing, and then generate debt, and sell debt, who create complicated derivatives that few understand and yet are traded for millions?
Jesus called them robbers.
Bankers are guilty of crimes against the people. So, let's describe them, as evidenced in the case histories that follow, crooked swindlers who seek any way to profit, however unethical, whose pinstriped suits have become a uniform of greed and lies, who receive millions in pay and even get paid hundreds of thousands of compensations when they take the coward's way out of a situation of their own creation and resign.

"Banking scandals are not new, but the scale and frequency of them in recent years is unprecedented." -
Howard Davies, Deputy Governor of the Bank of England

Now you can see why I left this to the end of the book - but read on. It's better than any novel as regards deceit and

Chapter Ten
Bankers & Robbers

corruption. This will strike a chord if you have been the victim of their incompetence and greed.

Let's go, for a sort of macabre fun, through a few of the recent scandals from the banking sector on both sides of the Atlantic.

Barclays Libor Swindle

One of the most significant scandals involving Barclays was the Libor scandal, which broke out in 2012. LIBOR stands for the London Interbank Offered Rate, the benchmark interest rate used to price financial products such as mortgages and loans. Barclays was one of several central banks that were accused of manipulating Libor rates to benefit their trading positions.

Barclays was fined £290 million ($450 million) by UK and US regulators for its involvement in the Libor scandal. The bank's CEO, Bob Diamond, and several other senior executives resigned after the scandal.

According to reports, **Bob Diamond's** total pay package for 2011 was around £17 million, which included a base salary of £1.35 million, a cash bonus of £2.7 million, and long-term incentives worth £12.8 million.

Bob Diamond is the epitome of the cunning banker who cares more for ego, cash and the short-term gratification of his shareholders than the victims of debt. Far removed the sort of person who should have been at the helm of a previously respectable bank.

Following the LIBOR scandal, Bob Diamond resigned. He was reportedly paid a severance package worth around £750,00 in addition to his outstanding bonus entitlements.

Chapter Ten
Bankers & Robbers

So, during his crooked control of Barclays, he smirkingly took home about £22 million (around $30 million), While others like Jane, a single mother, were struggling to feed herself and her children.

So, don't harbour any feeling of guilt when you close out your account without paying an iota if you are also struggling to put food on the table while paying excessive credit card debts in the way of compounding interest and fines while the likes of thieves such as Bob Diamond picked up over £22 million.

I sincerely hope you followed my advice and managed to eradicate your debt.

Another scandal involving Barclays was the **Qatar fundraising scandal, which also took place in 2012.** Barclays was accused of making secret payments to Qatar in exchange for investments in the bank during the 2008 financial crisis. The UK's Serious Fraud Office charged Barclays and four former executives with fraud concerning Qatar.

Wells Fargo fake accounts scandal (2016):
This scandal involved Wells Fargo employees opening fake accounts on behalf of customers without their consent to meet sales targets. The scandal resulted in a $185 million fine for Wells Fargo and the resignation of CEO John Stumpf.

When John Stumpf resigned, he forfeited approximately $41 million in unvested equity awards and retired without receiving a severance package. However, he still left the company with a retirement package and vested stock options valued at around $133.1 million.

HSBC money laundering scandal (2012):
HSBC (Hong Kong and Shanghai Banking Corporation) was

Chapter Ten
Bankers & Robbers

found to have processed transactions for Mexican drug cartels and other illegal organizations in violation of anti-money laundering laws. The scandal resulted in a $1.9 billion fine for HSBC.

UK: PPI miss-selling scandal (2000 to -2010):
Several UK banks were found to have mis-sold payment protection insurance (PPI) to customers, resulting in billions of pounds in compensation. The scandal affected banks, including Lloyds, Barclays, and RBS.

HBOS fraud scandal (2017)
(Halifax Bank of Scotland)
Several former executives of HBOS, a UK bank, were convicted of fraud and sentenced to prison for their roles in a scheme that involved fraudulent loans and kickbacks. The scandal resulted in losses of over £250 million for the bank.

Bank of America mortgage fraud settlement (2014)
Bank of America agreed to pay a record $16.65 billion to settle claims that it sold toxic mortgage-backed securities in the lead-up to the 2008 financial crisis.

Citigroup fraud settlement (2011)
Citigroup agreed to pay $285 million to settle charges that it misled investors about a complex mortgage investment product known as a collateralized debt obligation (CDO).

Deutsche Bank money laundering scandal (2017)
Deutsche Bank was fined $630 million by US and UK regulators for failing to prevent money laundering through its Moscow office.

Co-operative Bank crisis (2013)
The Co-operative Bank was found to have a capital shortfall of £1.5 billion, leading to the resignation of several senior

Chapter Ten
Bankers & Robbers

executives and a rescue deal that involved hedge funds taking control of the bank.

Tesco Bank cyber-attack (2016)
Tesco Bank suffered a cyber-attack that resulted in £2.5 million being stolen from customer accounts. The scandal caused by negligent security led to increased scrutiny of cybersecurity practices at banks.

Lloyds Bank fraud scandal (2017) :
Several former employees of HBOS, which Lloyds Bank had acquired, were convicted of a scheme that involved bribing small business owners to obtain fraudulent loans. The scandal resulted in several years of legal proceedings and compensation pay-outs for affected businesses.

The 2008 subprime mortgage crisis was a complex financial event that involved numerous parties, including lenders, borrowers, investors, regulators, and rating agencies. As a result, it is difficult to point to a single worst example of the crisis; many factors contributed to the widespread financial fallout.

However, one of the most notable and widely publicized examples of the subprime mortgage crisis was the collapse of Lehman Brothers, a major investment bank. Lehman Brothers had heavily invested in subprime mortgages and other risky assets. When the housing market collapsed and the value of these investments plummeted, Lehman Brothers found itself in financial trouble. Despite efforts to find a buyer or secure a government bailout, the company was ultimately forced to file for bankruptcy in September 2008, sending shockwaves throughout the global financial system and contributing to the onset of the Great Recession.

Chapter Ten
Bankers & Robbers

Another notable example of the subprime mortgage crisis was many lenders' widespread use of predatory lending practices. This included making loans to borrowers with poor credit histories and little ability to repay, offering adjustable-rate mortgages with low introductory rates that would reset to much higher rates later, and using deceptive or misleading tactics to lure borrowers into signing up for loans they did not fully understand. These practices contributed to a wave of foreclosures and defaults that ultimately undermined the stability of the housing market and the broader economy.

When referring to poor credit histories in the context of the subprime mortgage crisis, it generally means borrowers with a low credit score or a history of delinquent payments, bankruptcies, or other financial difficulties that would typically disqualify them from receiving traditional mortgage loans with favourable terms. As a result, these borrowers were often referred to as "subprime" borrowers and were seen as higher risk because of their poor credit histories.

Many subprime loans were made with adjustable rates, which allowed for low introductory rates that would reset to higher rates after a few years, making it difficult for borrowers to keep up with their payments. Additionally, many subprime loans were made with low or no down payment requirements, leaving borrowers with little equity in their homes and vulnerable to default if they experienced financial setbacks. These factors made subprime mortgages a high-risk investment for lenders and the broader financial system.

The penalties levied against bank directors for their role in the subprime mortgage crisis varied depending on the specific actions taken and the jurisdiction in which they operated. In some cases, directors faced legal action from regulators or civil lawsuits from investors or customers.

Chapter Ten
Bankers & Robbers

For example, in 2016, Wells Fargo reached a $185 million settlement with regulators over allegations that the bank had opened millions of unauthorized accounts for its customers. The settlement included a $100 million fine levied by the Consumer Financial Protection Bureau, the largest fine ever imposed by the agency at the time. In addition, the bank's CEO, John Stumpf, was forced to resign and forfeit $41 million in stock awards.

In other cases, bank directors faced criminal charges or other legal penalties for their role in the crisis. For example, in 2012, a jury found two former Bear Stearns hedge fund managers guilty of securities fraud related to managing two funds that invested heavily in subprime mortgages. The managers were sentenced to prison terms of 42 months and 24 months, respectively.

However, it is worth noting that many bank directors and executives were not held personally accountable for their role in the crisis. As a result, some faced little to no legal or financial consequences for their actions. The lack of accountability for those responsible for the crisis has been a source of criticism and controversy in the years since.

AND ... were you ever worried about dumping your loan and walking free?

Just this once. I hope not.

Yarns of banks & cards & other bits

These are two case histories. To avoid clutter, I did not add to the main body of the book.

They are, however, truly fascinating and further reinforce my conclusions that bankers are pragmatic, lazy, and sometimes stupid and how to use that to your advantage.

Harry and the Story of Multiple Card Debts

This is an incredible story about a friend who got into debt and couldn't pay, and more importantly, how he naively got out of it. (I have changed his name for privacy reasons.)

It's so macabre and out of the norm that I did not want to include this saga, or perhaps fable, in the book's main body because it is not, I think typical - yet, word for word, utterly true.

It does reinforce my point about banks being heartless bastards who are more interested in profit than right or wrong, so here it is - as an appendage on the final pages - read on; it's interesting.

"So, Harry, you came into the office of Barclays Bank and shot the manager dead? Shame.
No matter, we just need to replace the desk, all that blood – no matter its insured, now, can you pay anything off the debt before your trial and incarceration? Remember, we are here to help."

Just teasing...

Back to the story:
Around ten years ago Harry was in litigation due to an intestacy dispute - he lost. Of course, he tells me, he shouldn't have lost. Of course not. No person on this planet goes to court, loses, pays all the costs, and agrees with the judgment. And I agreed with him - the finding was most unfair.
The upshot, however, and the point of this story is he ended up £90,000 in debt to his solicitors and the courts. Bless them.

To service this debt, he feverishly applied for and obtained about ten credit cards; so far, so easy. He doesn't even remember exactly how many. Nearly all of them offered a maximum of around a £10,000 credit limit.

Over the following few years, he sold assets, made money, and reduced the total debt to around £60,000. But one day, in the frigid light of dawn, he realized he had no further assets to sell and could no longer keep up with monthly payments from his income.

He wrote to all the card companies, and then the agencies for some of them had already sold the debt, offering to pay what he could afford each month, just an affordable fraction, of what he owed, on the condition that they froze the interest.

He clarified that all had to agree; otherwise, he would default on all of them. He bluffed he would seek bankruptcy if they pushed him.

They all agreed to his offer. No other practical choice for them. For the next few years, he managed the agreed monthly payments.
However, he hit hard times again.

Exasperated, emotionally exhausted and beaten, he offered a token payment of £1 per month to each company, believing it was a sign of good faith - a bad move - saying he had no means to pay more.

He made it clear it was not an offer; it was what he would do – accept or reject. By accepting, the creditors knew that, at best, they kept the debt active and free from the statute of limitations. They also realized that was all they would ever get, and further negotiations were futile. I asked him about this while writing this book - was he still paying £1 a month to each card company? He replied, "No, I don't think so," he had forgotten about it. So, it seems, had the card companies. This is an incredible story, and a lot of conclusions can be drawn from it

They were realistic. They got back 30% of the original debts plus interest and then further payments, which they may have lost if the account went delinquent. Thus, by accepting £1 a month, they kept the statute of limitations away - the debt is still technically active.

Yarns of banks & cards & other bits

If he won the lottery or married a millionairess, they could still prosecute.

Both scenarios are very unlikely.

"Carpe diem - enjoy life, seize the day, do not waste any more time."

And enjoy your coffee

Peter, the HSBC & the Gizmo

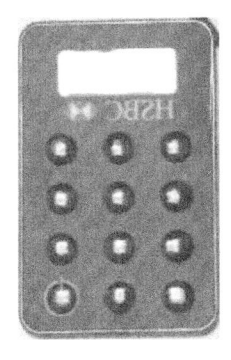

Another example of how banks react and dispose of anything that could cause them extra work, thought, or even customer service.
This is a valuable insight into banks' psyche and preferred methodology.

Peter was my neighbour when I was in France. He had moved there about ten years ago.

He kept his British account with the HSBC bank in England and also a British telephone that was registered with the HSBC.

To access his account, he had to use a sort of device that you held near the computer and pressed buttons. They called it a 'Secure Key'. Very clever when it worked.

Shortly after Brexit, he tried to access his account, but the secure key was dead. He tried to go online to report the failed device via the *'chat with a friendly operative'* function. He could not unless he was logged in as a customer. He could not log in without the Secure Key.

He tried to call the help centre located in some third-world country. After a long wait, some disinterested person who had not listened said she would have to create a telephone access password. Before he could say anything, the line switched to nauseating music, and she did not return to the phone.

Several tries and one hour later he was told that he could only access his account with his 'Secure Key'. He patiently explained that it did not work. She said that he could get a new one by following the instructions on the company website

He tried, but they needed confirmation of his identity. To facilitate that they would send a passcode to his telephone.

Unfortunately, since Brexit, it did not work. He was told to log in to his account to update his phone records. Exasperated, he repeated he could log in to his account without the Secure Key.

So, recap: (This could be a script for a pantomime.)

- He could not get online without a Secure Key to check his account (he guessed he was about £800 overdrawn).
- He could not get a replacement Secure Key without a telephone.
- He could not amend his phone number without a secure key
- He could not access chat messages without logging in, and he could not log in without the Secure Key.
- There was no published email address.
- The call centre was worse than useless. Disinterested and not in the least willing to help.

He then received a standard stereotyped letter from HSBC to his French address confirming that his account was overdrawn and requesting payment.

There was no way to respond over the internet as his account was not accessible, and thus so were communications.

After the Brexit debacle, letters take up to six weeks from the EU to the UK. and visa-versa. So, he typed out a letter fully describing the problem and emailed it to a friend in the UK, who printed and posted it to the bank.

No reply.

He sent a second letter, this time by recorded delivery. Still no reply.

He sent a third letter, this time addressed, both on the letter and the envelope:

> "The janitor, caretaker, even the manager, or anyone, please, who would take the time to read and reply."

At last, he received an email from one of the senior clerks asking how she could help.

He explained in detail how he wanted to keep the account and maintain the balance within their rules.

He insisted that he wanted to be able to check his account. She said she could not send him a new 'Secure Key' unless he could verify himself via his registered telephone. He again explained that he no longer had that number.

Then he received a letter telling him his account was closed. Obviously, within the bank, there was no liaison between the friendly clerk who was in email contact and the accounts department with a finger on the 'send horrible letters' button.

In exasperation, he sent a reply email in which he wrote, "Do you want this account to go delinquent? I will not pay anything if I cannot check the payments, charges, debits, and balance."

She essentially said, "Okay," - and promptly closed the account.

They would not circumvent their rule regarding the Secure Key and phone.

Yarns of banks & cards & other bits

Maybe it was a security loophole that no one other than senior executives could amend. It was probably cheaper to write off the £800 than convene a board meeting, with the necessary majority of directors, amend the security protocols, re-draft, re-print, and distribute to every customer.

A month later received a letter saying if he paid 2/3 of the account, they would accept it as 'full and final'.
Obviously, another department was not liaising and trying for whatever they could get. Or perhaps more likely, the letter was spewed out by a computer.

He ignored it.
Since then, no further communication.
Nor begging letters from a debt collection agency.
End of story.

Chapter Twelve

Epilogue

Readers, good people who have found themselves on the wrong side of the rich/poor divide are now paying exorbitant interest rates and fines to subsidize those people who are already well off. For people to be rich, you need people to be poor.

There will always be in a monitory society a conflict of interest. The seller v the buyer—the lender v the borrower.

Yes, of course, you should have ensured your wage, pension or savings covered your living cost.
But it did not. You are not in control of prices.

So, you sign up for a credit card or start using cards you hardly used before. When you can't pay the current month's purchases, interest is added, then the following month, your purchases exceed what you can afford to pay, so you pay what you can afford, then more interest is added to the debt, and so on, interest compounding until your card is maxed out.

Now you have no spending power left on your card. Just a liability adding more to your living costs, and monthly bills you did not have before.

Each time you swipe your card on those machines you go further into debt.

While I acknowledge that it's not fair to renege on debts, I question whether it's fair for people like Jane, a single mother struggling to make ends meet, to be burdened with debt by market greed - while Bob Diamond scoffs.

Chapter Twelve
Epilogue

The exact number of foreclosures in the USA during the 2008 banking crisis, a making caused by the greed of bankers, is difficult to determine, but an estimated 7.3 million homes were foreclosed in this time due to a range of factors, but mostly the subprime mortgage debacle; banks creating money to create debts and then selling debts.

I remain hopeful that a fairer society can be achieved one day. Single mothers like Jane are more valuable to a community than crooked bankers

Do I feel bad about telling you the tricks to get out of the stranglehold of debt?

No, I do not when children are sent home to die in some countries because their parents can't afford the fees.
When pensioners, people who should be revered, not disdained, get into debt because they can't afford basics like food, clothing, and heating.
When hotels boast penthouse suites at $10,000 a night while good people in unfortunate circumstances sleep on the streets below.
When nurses, teachers and hard-working contributors to society, the value producers, not value destroyers, struggle with the cost of living while the CEOs of INCs and PLCs pocket millions.
When there is a better level of social justice and a better level of social conscience - a level of civilisation that's still a dream - then I will repent.

You may not follow the advice in this book. Or, you may follow with some with caution – as you should.

Chapter Twelve
Epilogue

Whatever, I hope you have learned something about the crooked world of banks and debt. The cause of this is the grossly uneven distribution of wealth fuelled by greed.

What can the bankers do? Do they have an alternative other than chasing delinquent debt?
Well, yes, they do. They could confiscate the millions they paid the likes of Bob Diamond and distribute that to the neediest of their debtors, the pensioners, the parents of sick children, and the homeless.

I rest my case:

I hope this book has helped you. I hope it has given you another chance to rebuild your life.
Lend it to your friends if they have similar problems or are just interested in what you are doing and how you're coping.

I find it irritating when I see on the title pages of some books a notice then that it 'can't be lent or otherwise shared.' What nonsense! I will share the book I paid for with whom I want – and that should be seen as a compliment, not the cause of a prohibition.

So, dear reader, please share this book when and where you want, in your blogs, social media or whatever.

Chapter Twelve
Epilogue

If this book has helped you then it will help others. So, I am asking you a favour. It takes about three minutes to post a comment on Amazon. Give your opinion – about this book, about the state of society, the bankers, the debt 'industry' and its prey – or just say 'hi'.

I leave you to decide on the star rating – not for my politics, that would be unfair either way – but the information, the style.

Okay, the little box where you can leave your comment is on the lower section of the Amazon book's page. Currently a white box on a white background.
So, a tiny bit of scrolling to find.

I also welcome your views by direct contact via email - good or bad. If you have questions let me know your experience. Did you get out of debt the 'Jail Break' way? What, if any, problems did you encounter? Was it smooth? How do you feel now?

I will be pleased to help you. Write to me confident I will never disclose or sell your identity. I will reply to your email with care, thought and suggestions.
Also, as promised earlier, when my next book is published, I

Chapter Twelve
Epilogue

will send you a link to get, for the first ten days, a free Kindle or a paperback copy at a special launch price.

My email address is:

Charles@LiteraryCat.org

Ciao, have an excellent, debt-free, happy life from now on.

Check out some of the books in the next section.

I am thinking of you.

Charles

LiteraryCat.org
Publishers & Freelance Writers

Credits.
I want to thank Pixabay.com and Pexels.com for their graphics and photos supplied by freelance photographers and artists.
Particularly the cover photo, albeit much edited, of the protesting woman by Tima Miroshnichenko via Pexels

Further Reading

To follow are some books I recommend.

As an author, I have an affiliate account with Amazon. This means I will earn a small commission if you buy a book. Just check them out for now and read the first 10% for free.

Wealth consists not in having great possessions,
but in having few wants
Epictetus

Further Reading

Hi again, the first couple of books on the list is advice on how to stay out of debt. Good sound advice. Basically, paying what you owe, somehow, and then being sensible - of course good advice and worth checking out (Hoping by now, of course, you have ditched your - ex-debt - with the bankers.)

How to Get Out of Debt, Stay Out of Debt, and Live Prosperously:
Based on the Proven Principles and Techniques of Debtors Anonymous

The more conventional way to get out of debt and stay that way. J.J.M.

Getting Out Of Debt - Money Management
You Cannot Afford to Wait Any Longer
Rich or Poor 9 Simple Rules to Clear Your Debts Faster, Rebuild Your Credit
Michael Steven

Different advice from my book.
Worth reading, for a different approach, albeit
Quite pricey for 124 pages. J.J.M.

And to follow some books on the psychology of wealth, and happiness, creation.

I have been rich - I have been poor – I prefer rich every time.

Money does not make you happy.
Believe me, don't kid yourself,
nor does poverty. Only the rich tell you that.
Universal quotes.

Further Reading

Think and Grow Rich
Napoleon Hill

Think and Grow Rich has been called the "Granddaddy of All Motivational Literature." It was the first book to boldly ask, "What makes a winner?" The man who asked and listened for the answer, Napoleon Hill, is now counted in the top ranks of the world's winners himself.

The Lazy Man's Way to Riches
DYNA/PSYC
Everything in the World You Really Want!

I first read this a long time ago. The principles of instructing your subconscious to give you the wealth, love & status you deserve. And it works. A simple, practical read. Well recomended.

This can be expensive on Amazon. Search the internet for free PDF version J.J.M.

To follow the most important of all books to read. Books on improving your spiritual being - Happiness is a choice. Make it your choice.

The Power of Your Subconscious Mind,
Dr. Joseph Murphy

Dr. Joseph Murphy gives you the tools you need to unlock the awesome powers of your subconscious mind. You can improve your relationships, your finances, your physical well-being.

The Journey
A Practical Guide to Healing Your Life and Setting Yourself Free

Join the hundreds of thousands worldwide who have since used The Journey to awaken their own infinite potential and set themselves free. The Journey is a powerful, step-by-step means to find direct access to the soul, the infinite intelligence that is within us all.

Further Reading

EyMiSo
A Radically New Approach to
Unleash the Power of your Subconscious Mind

It widely accepted that the subconscious mind when free of from the ego, clutter and erroneous messages submitted by the conscious mind will, by proper instruction, make certain that you will gain everything you could imagine.

The Power of Now:
A Guide to Spiritual Enlightenment
Eckhart Tolle

To make the journey into The Power of Now you need to leave your analytical mind and its false created self, the ego, behind. Access to the Now is everywhere - in the body, the silence, and the space all around you.

Awaken the Giant Within

I know that no matter where you are in your life, you want more! No matter how well you're already doing or how challenged you now may be, deep inside you there lies a belief that your experience of life can and will be much greater than it already is. You are destined for your own unique form of greatness."

To follow are some books you may enjoy.
Radical and refreshing thoughts.

Further Reading

The Simulated Multiverse:
An MIT Computer Scientist Explores Parallel Universes, the Simulation Hypothesis, Quantum Computing and the Mandela Effect

Life After the State:
Why We Don't Need Government
Dominic Frisby
Have you ever had the nagging feeling that the problems the country faces are spiralling out of control, that the government has lost its way and that, despite its promises, nothing ever changes?

Nomad Capitalist
Reclaim Your Freedom with Offshore Companies, Dual Citizenship, Foreign Banks, and Overseas Investments
The world has changed forever. Governments have expanded their reach over their citizens' lives. Power is being consolidated by an elite few. The world economy has become more volatile and unpredictable. Meanwhile, the internet, a globalizing world economy, and the emergence of the developing world all present opportunities

Further Reading

Thank You

Notes

Always a few blank pages to follow due to the way print books are produced - so feel free to scribble.

Printed in Great Britain
by Amazon